T0331077

"I highly endorse this book as an exciting resource for navigating the challenges of today's rapidly changing and uncertain business landscape. By combining evolutionary biology and management theory, the authors offer a fresh perspective on enterprise transformation and change. They emphasise the importance of recognizing organisations as fundamentally human systems and propose the concept of organisational evolvability as a guiding framework. The book covers a range of crucial topics, including distinguishing between complicated and complex, embracing emergent change, and operationalizing evolvability through a sense-adapt-respond loop. It also addresses sensemaking gaps, scaling approaches, and measuring outcomes in complex conditions. This book is a must-read for leaders and practitioners seeking to enhance their organisation's adaptability and thrive in a dynamic environment".

Emmanuel Bucallie, *Head of Platforms and Transformation,*
Bank of Singapore, Singapore

"My first encounter with Sunil, as YOOX's new Co-General Manager, was unforgettable. Tasked with leading an '(Agile) Transformation,' I quickly learned the enormity of the challenge. My question about its duration was met with Sunil's enlightening, 'Never, Irene. It never ends.' This book distils lessons I encountered in my leadership journey and introduces new insights for thriving in change. It underscores evolvability and continuous learning as keys to success, offering real-life examples and actionable frameworks. A valuable resource, I'm eager to share it with fellow leaders. Thank you Zhen and Sunil for this enlightening gift".

Irene Boni, *Board member, Angel Investor, Italy*

"Evolution, Enterprise, and Transformation - all of these are complex subjects by itself. Combining those three with a single purpose is even harder. This book from Sunil Mundra is a gem filled with a practical approach to achieving transformation in an enterprise. This book effortlessly brings all three together with a logical sequence and explanation along the way to achieve the same. This is a must-read book for courageous leaders aiming to transform the business in the complex business world today".

Mahesh Baxi, *Go-founder and CEO at Provus Inc., USA*

"A definitive must-read for those dedicated to guiding their organisations towards a sustainable future. Sunil and Zhen present a compelling argument that authentic organisational agility does not hinge solely on periodic technological updates, but rather on ingraining a culture of perpetual adaptation and evolution deep within the organisation's DNA. In today's tumultuous business landscape, leaders will find an indispensable guide within these pages. Offering profound insights, the book illuminates pathways for organisations to not just survive but thrive, through the cultivation of adaptability, experimentation, and continuous learning".

Thierry Thibault, *Managing Director, Societe Generale Insurance, Germany*

"As a venture builder, I recognize the critical importance of designing organisations that can thrive in uncertainty. This book offers a powerful framework for entrepreneurial leaders seeking to create adaptable, resilient companies. By embracing the principles of evolvability – rapid experimentation, decentralised decision-making, and continuous learning – startups can become living organisms that evolve in harmony with their environment. The authors provide actionable insights for fostering cultures of innovation and building businesses that can scale without losing their entrepreneurial essence. An essential guide for any founder looking to build enduring ventures in a world of constant disruption".

Arunthep Sangvareethip, *Founder/CEO/Venture Builder, Emetworks, Thailand*

"Enterprise transformation is an ongoing journey for all organisations. Having worked with Sunil on various projects, his insights on how such transformation can be managed or orchestrated is a must read for C Suite leaders as it provides new perspectives on how various parts of an organisation are interconnected as a larger, more complex ecosystem that is constantly changing. Leaders must understand and be equipped with the right mindset on how they can best manage constant change to steer their organisations successfully in today's volatile landscape".

Nicholas Lee, *CEO, EZ-Link, Singapore*

"Both a former colleague and master in complexity theory and practice, Zhen offers a profound exploration in *Evolvability in Business* shedding light on the imperative themes of transformation in our increasingly complex world. Through her insightful introduction of the term 'evolvability,' Zhen prompts readers to contemplate the adaptive capabilities of organizations, teams, and challenging subjects. In this illuminating work, Zhen navigates the intricate terrain of decision-making amidst a plethora of established and emerging methodologies, urging readers to discern what best aligns with the current moment and context. She deftly guides us through complex concepts, such as the Vector Theory of Change, disciplined nesting, sensemaking gaps, and organisational debt, all while addressing the omnipresent concerns of scale and measuring change once it occurs. Zhen's narrative is akin to a captivating dialogue with a cherished mentor. Her rare ability to translate powerful concepts with clarity and precision imbues the reading experience with the joy of learning from a trusted teacher. *Evolvability in Business* is not merely informative; it is an inspirational journey that propels readers to delve deeper into the realms of enterprise transformation. With Zhen as our guide, the path forward is both enlightening and invigorating".

Ian Macdonald, *Head of Applied Complexity, Itau Bank, Brazil*

"Change and transformation feature strongly in all business conversations today. Changes come faster, bigger, and are more interconnected and unpredictable now than ever before. How we respond and manage through constant uncertainty provide the competitive advantage for leaders and organisations. As a person who makes a living helping companies navigate this journey, I believe having a strong understanding of complexity theory, the perspective it offers, and the unique tools it provides leaders is essential to success. This is why I am so grateful for the insights that I have gained from my relationship with Zhen Goh. We have spent countless hours exploring these topics, and I have learned so much from her about the concepts and applications of these methods. For many people the complexity perspective is intuitive and clear. For others it is a struggle. Those people lucky enough to find this book will now have access to the same insights explained in simple, clear, and practical terms. This book is a beacon for leadership success, and I will be making it a key recommendation to the business leaders with whom I work".

David William Lee, *Change Leader and Consultant &*
Managing Director, Prosci, Singapore

"Change and transformation are ubiquitous to business. But so too are the seemingly intractable issues that come with it. This book provides a refreshing new perspective on how to create organic, sustainable change, blending academic insights, management theory and corporate experience to give leaders a guide to the right attitude and approaches needed to truly engage with the human systems that make up their organisations. While many of the ideas in the book may seem intuitive – listening to your people and meeting them where they are, for example – they are rarely put into practice effectively. The book will challenge existing views on transformation, help make you comfortable with embracing uncertainty, and ultimately leave you with a new set of tools to enable enterprise transformation".

Nitish Upadhyaya, *Director of Behavioral Insights, London, UK*

Evolvability in Business

Through the unique combination of evolutionary biology and management theory applied to business cases, and keeping in mind that organisations are fundamentally human systems, Goh and Mundra propose organisational evolvability as a new frame to guide enterprise transformation and change.

Some of the topics covered in the book include: Understanding the differences between Complicated and Complex; Moving from Planned Change to Emergent Change; Applying principles of evolution to enterprise evolvability, and how to operationalise it using a Sense-Adapt-respond loop; Identifying and addressing Sensemaking gaps; including different approaches to scaling and repaying organisational debt; Measuring outcomes under conditions of complexity. This book proposes that transformation is not a one-and-done event but a continuous process of adapting to a dynamic and unpredictable environment. The goal of transformation should be to enhance organisational evolvability – the capacity of a system for adaptive evolution. This book encourages leaders and practitioners to view organisations as open and complex adaptive systems and provides frameworks that help them to manage transformations with adaptive grace.

A perfect volume for managers, executives and leaders at companies of all sizes. It will also be of interest to instructors in executive education, as well as scholars in organisational studies and business management. This book is for anyone seeking to create a culture of adaptability and change.

Zhen Goh is Founder of The Emerginarium. She has close to 20 years of experience in applying sensemaking and complexity, and co-authored *Cynefin: Weaving Sense-making into the Fabric of our World*. She believes that "knowledge is a martial art", and is passionate about supporting just and meaningful transitions.

Sunil Mundra is a seasoned professional with an exceptional track record in driving Transformation and Organizational Change. He is the author of the best-selling book *Enterprise Agility – Being Agile in a Changing World*. His current area of interest is working with senior leaders to enable them to enhance agility in their enterprises to deal more effectively with a highly disruptive and complex environment.

Routledge-Solaris Applied Research in Business Management and Board Governance
Series Editor: Charles Phua

Professional Management Consulting
A Guide for New and Emerging Consultants
Alan J. Blackman

Evolvability in Business
Enterprise Transformation in an Age of Complexity
Zhen Goh and Sunil Mundra

For more information about this series, please visit: www.routledge.com/Routledge-Solaris-Applied-Research-in-Business-Management-and-Board-Governance/book-series/RSARB

ZHEN GOH AND SUNIL MUNDRA

Evolvability in Business
Enterprise Transformation in an Age of Complexity

Routledge
Taylor & Francis Group

LONDON AND NEW YORK

Designed cover image: Unna Yarles

First published 2025
by Routledge
4 Park Square, Milton Park, Abingdon, Oxon, OX14 4RN

and by Routledge
605 Third Avenue, New York, NY 10158

Routledge is an imprint of the Taylor & Francis Group, an informa business

© 2025 Zhen Goh and Sunil Mundra

British Library Cataloguing-in-Publication Data
A catalogue record for this book is available from the British Library

Library of Congress Cataloging-in-Publication Data
Names: Goh, Zhen, author. | Mundra, Sunil, author.
Title: Evolvability in business : enterprise transformation in an age of
complexity / Zhen Goh and Sunil Mundra.
Description: Abingdon, Oxon ; New York, NY : Routledge, 2025. | Series:
Routledge-Solaris applied research in business management and board
governance | Includes bibliographical references and index. Identifiers:
LCCN 2024022479 (print) | LCCN 2024022480 (ebook) | ISBN
9781032826349 (hardcover) | ISBN 9781032826172 (paperback) | ISBN
9781003505433 (ebook)
Subjects: LCSH: Organizational change. | Organizational resilience. |
Organizational sociology.
Classification: LCC HD58.8 .G6184 2025 (print) | LCC HD58.8 (ebook) |
DDC 658.4/06--dc23/eng/20240503
LC record available at https://lccn.loc.gov/2024022479
LC ebook record available at https://lccn.loc.gov/2024022480

ISBN: 978-1-032-82634-9 (hbk)
ISBN: 978-1-032-82617-2 (pbk)
ISBN: 978-1-003-50543-3 (ebk)

DOI: 10.4324/9781003505433

Typeset in Joanna
by SPi Technologies India Pvt Ltd (Straive)

Contents

FIGURES

TABLES

Introduction

A recount of the past half decade would leave anyone dizzy.

In 2019, the Covid-19 virus took the world hostage for a period. Everyone had to take refuge in their homes in our bid to socially distance. The disruption to our social organisation and activities also revealed the fragility of our supply chains, and the dysfunctions in our remuneration systems for "essential workers". The macro-disruptions impacted broader patterns of work-life, and set off a Great Reshuffle, where workers began quitting their jobs en masse and seeking out better working arrangements. Mental health and well-being became suitable employee demands. At this moment, China is still trying to find its way forward as it awakens from the self-isolation caused by its zero-Covid policies.

The Russia-Ukraine war continues; and the Hamas-Israel conflict has again destabilised the Middle East region.

In 2023, we experienced a slew of confusing and theoretically contradictory macroeconomic signals. In Europe and the US, there was an economic downturn combined with record low unemployment and massive labour shortages. We experienced a surge of inflation which raised prices of almost everything, and yet consumers continued spending. This also led to a period of escalating interest rates and costs of capital that signalled an end to the period of "cheap money".

We wrote this book alongside the investment bubble surrounding generative AI and large language models. It presented many foundational challenges to how we should think about education and the future of work. We cannot deny that it also presented some existential challenges to the role of scholarship and this very book.

We have undergone a fundamental shift change.

In a Financial Times article, published 16 February 2023, furniture giant IKEA announced that it has shed traditional budgeting to focus

DOI: 10.4324/9781003505433-1

on "scenario planning" instead as its leadership has recognised that the traditional tools it used to employ that gave them margins of error by 0.3% are no longer useful. All the economic theory their forecasting models had been built on were no longer effective after the pandemic. Now, instead of setting specific goals for the year, IKEA sets out a series of potential scenarios that allows the business wiggle room as the outlook changes. It acknowledges that wide different outcomes are possible. Jesper Brodin, the Managing Director of IKEA remarked, "Look at what people have gone through: The pandemic, the economic damage, the tragedy of war, energy prices… What people might have underestimated is human resilience" [1].

It is this very remarkable aspect of "human" that we will focus on in this book – human systems and the complex adaptive systems they are a part of, create, and, which in turn, influences them. These come together to create the conditions that any enterprise transformation navigates. Our efforts at transforming any business ecosystem need to match the resilience of human systems. We propose a framework and philosophy of evolvability – emphasising a focus on enhancing a system's capability for adaptive diversity – to better support an organisation's capability to transform in a manner that retains its ability to strategically respond to change in an age of increasing uncertainty.

DIGITAL TRANSFORMATION AND DISRUPTIVE INNOVATION

Back in 1995, Clayton Christensen and his collaborators had already called out that companies would be feeling the impact of disruptive innovation on their businesses, and that resilient business strategies would need to be guided by an awareness of the ever-persistent threat of disruption [2]. In Christensen's words, before his untimely passing in 2020, "disruptive innovation describes a process by which a product or service powered by a technology enabler initially takes root in simple applications at the low end of a market — typically by being less expensive and more accessible — and then relentlessly moves upmarket, eventually displacing established competitors" [3]. A review of 65 million papers, patents and software products that spanned the 60 year timeframe of 1954 to 2014 identified disruptive science and technological advances as one of the strongest influencers of disruption [4]. The impact of technology driven disruptions is universal, and can be observed across industries and geographies. Traditional entry barriers based on physical assets have been slowly eroding for decades. Netflix, WhatsApp and Uber are taken-for-granted everyday systems we use that exemplify these new age enterprises that have broken traditional entry barriers. These same technological advancements have also led to customers becoming more empowered and demanding. Through consumers' greater awareness of choices available to them, and the power of social media, the pressure on enterprises to transform and evolve to stay relevant has never been greater.

The Information Age ushered in monumental changes. This has been further augmented by the Digital Age that has enabled enterprises to leverage new technologies to accelerate their learning and consumer reach. Technology improves not only how enterprises can better design products and services, but also continuously improve on customer experience and delight, and speed to market. The organisations that began rapid adoption of digital technology, as well as an IT-driven strategy early have enjoyed the benefits. The ones who did not have been in a scramble to catch up. As a result of this, a casual poke around almost any industry will reveal that most organisations are undergoing some kind of Agile or Digital transformation. However, in the same vein, the casual poking around will also reveal "various studies from academics, consultants, and analysts indicate that the rate of digital transformations failing to meet their original objectives ranges from 70% to 95%" [5].

This book is not about digital transformation, but it acknowledges the current trends in transformation and discusses organisation transformation whilst addressing digital examples. It speaks to digital transformation as a wave that sits within broader transformation efforts.

WHAT THIS BOOK IS ABOUT

In this book, we provide new thinking and framing that will enable enterprises across industries and sectors to deal with accelerating changes and uncertainty. Through the unique combination of evolutionary biology, human sciences and management theory applied to business cases, we propose organisational evolvability as a new frame to guide enterprise transformation and change. The intent is to provide a broader framing mechanism that will then be able to support different methods and approaches based on each enterprise's context, needs and existing proficiencies. Rather than a step-by-step playbook, we discuss examples and frameworks that can guide leaders and change-makers to plan and act differently.

We posit that the "failure" of most transformation efforts stem from subscribing to a traditional belief that transformation is about evolving from one state of organisation to another, and achieving objectives that would mark the arrival of the desired transformed state. This is the "Transformation Myth" [6] as has been described by the award-winning book of the same title. Transformation is not a "one-walk dog" – you cannot walk the dog once, and expect the job to be done. Transformation is "not a one-and-done event, but a continuous process of adapting to a volatile and uncertain environment" [6].

In Chapter One, we challenge this traditional view of transformation and emphasise the importance of focusing on evolvability instead – that is, building an enterprise that constantly learns, adapts, and evolves to survive and thrive in a dynamic world. Successful enterprise transformation hinges on evolvability: The ability to continuously adjust and respond to change, rather than simply pursuing specific goals.

Traditional transformation approaches that address individual parts or specific metrics often fall short because they overlook the interconnectedness and complexity of the enterprise. Instead, transformation efforts should view the enterprise as a living entity constantly in flux, requiring continuous adaptation.

The chapter identifies several key elements for successful transformation:

- Monitor organisational health: Track not only business outcomes but also adaptability and agility through measures like decision-making speed and regular evaluations.
- Bridge the gap between local and system optimisation: Don't just focus on localised improvements; connect them to broader organisational considerations.
- Cultivate a culture of learning and innovation: Encourage experimentation, learn from mistakes, and embrace the iterative nature of transformation.

We will explore this need for constant adaptation by recognising organisations as complex adaptive systems; which are nested within even more complex constellations of systems. The metaphor that has become common in describing these webs of interdependencies and systems dynamics is that of evolution and ecosystems. It is a welcome transition, away from the metaphor of closed, stable state systems of machines and engines, into recognising the open, complex and organic nature of our human systems. In this chapter, we also distil the literature and science behind the field of evolutionary biology that we borrow the ecosystem and evolvability metaphors from.

In complex systems, any action or intervention creates change and consequences in the system, whether intended or otherwise. We react to intervention and our systems change irreversibly, and so do we. We are never able to "go back to normal". The baseline for "normal" changes and adapts, much as we are now discovering after Covid-19's disruptions.

The question arises, then, whether transformation outcomes can be measured in such simplistic and binary ways, as either success or failure. When we dig further, even Christensen's disruptive innovation theory of change reveals arbitrary definitions of success. In his original research on the Disk-Drive industry in the 1980s, Christensen had established the arbitrary cutoff for measuring success as firms who had constantly achieved more than fifty million dollars in revenues in any single year between 1977 and 1989 – even if they subsequently withdrew from the market [7]. This definition privileges short-term outputs and business outcomes, and ignores the need for managing on-going transformation that enhances survival and sustainability of enterprise.

In Chapter 2, we discuss the need to move away from planned approaches to emergent approaches when dealing in complexity. The chapter addresses the key differences between complicated and complex scenarios, and discusses core properties of Complex Adaptive Systems (CAS). In this discussion, we review traditional planned approaches to enterprise transformation (i.e. Big Bang, Incubator and Phasing), and highlight some of their limitations.

We also introduce new approaches that are better suited for emergent change as these approaches factor in the need for adaptation and shorter feedback loops. Examples of these are:

- Vector-based theory of change: With focus on identifying potential directions and "stepping stones" for change rather than defining a fixed end state.

- Disciplined nesting: Managing multiple initiatives within the transformation journey and coordinating resource flow to support emergent activities which can contribute to the overall direction.

Human systems are in constant adaptation, and any plan or model of the system is also, just a snap-shot in time of something in constant evolution. In Chapter 2, we describe how this has an implication on how we "road-map" our transformation journeys.

Transformation efforts are costly in terms of time, resources, attention and discomfort. Careful time and effort needs to be invested in trying to roadmap the journey, and define linked objectives. These provide guidelines that can discipline the effort. These objectives are often articulated as leaders strive to get the outcome of "successful transformation". Transformation is an on-going and adaptive affair, and as the title of Chapter Two tells us, "there is your roadmap, and then there is what really happens". Dwight Eisenhower, the US President who created the Interstate Highway System and Departments of Health, Education and Welfare, famously said "Plans are worthless, but planning is everything".

Any roadmap or plan which was designed in advance is often incorrect, but the planning process is still critical as it is an exploration of options, contingencies and potential threats. This process of probing helps us to understand what to do when things inevitably do not go to plan as the uncertainty of the future presents itself – it enhances our evolvability, and the evolvability of the transformation plan. Whatever roadmaps we develop in our planning processes provide guiding frameworks at best, but transformation requires us to stay attentive to the ever-changing present, and be flexible and responsive.

This leads us into Chapter 3, which goes deeper into the concept of enterprise evolvability and talks about how an organisation can enhance their evolvability. It reviews the four key forces of evolution, and speak to how organisations can leverage these as guidelines to design their own approaches. These are (1) *allowing for mutation* by communicating a clear strategic intent together with the right latitude and enabling constraints put in place to allow the system to interpret the change, whilst self-correcting against the intent; (2) *stimulating gene flow* by developing a networked and ecosystem approach where ideas, agents and resources are free to flow across the system; (3) *natural selection* implies that the company ecosystem is in and of itself a collective prediction market. With the right environment in place, talent and interest tend to pool around good ideas and drain from bad ones; Last, (4) *genetic drift* refers to "the change in frequency of an existing variant in the population due to chance - that is, not all ideas or projects that were successful in the past will remain so, and the next mutation might take us by surprise. We, therefore, need to maintain mechanisms that allow for weak signal detection so we can exploit early patterns, as well as plan ahead for any early signals of "drifting".

Utilising case studies, we discuss organisational design principles that enhance for these conditions. We also introduce the *Sense-Adapt-respond* loop that can help to support the operationalisation of an evolvable organisation.

- Sense: This involves incorporating diversity of perspectives across the system, and openness in allowing for creation and evolution of new meaning and understanding that will impact on how we frame the business.
- Adapt: Affording the system and its agents the nimbleness and flexibility to make changes, and self-organise to realign priorities.
- respond: Ability of the system to respond when the adaptive move has been identified.

In Chapter 4, we address the practical constraint of transformation often being unevenly experienced and distributed. Change and transformation are seldom neat nor linear. Organisations always present un-uniform coalitions of the willing, and of the resistant, and of the poorly executed. This results in gaps and debts. Transformation requires a sincere willingness to make payments on those debts, and planning to more effectively pay forward. In this chapter, we discuss two types of debt that we need to be mindful of. The first is "organisational debt", a term coined by Steve Blank that was used to describe "all the people/ culture compromises made to 'just get it done' in the early stages of startup". He had compared it to "technical debt" which refers to an accumulation of old code and short term solutions for a digital product that if left unpaid, collectively accrues into performance burden. Much like traditional debt, it has to be paid back — either in a proper refactoring of code, or with a lot of money.

"Organisational debt is like technical debt - but worse" [8], as often-times the debt is ignored, unacknowledged or worked around until it is too late. Whilst the initial article was focused on the debt that start-ups incur as they grow, the term has found resonance in trans-formation management. As Aaron Dignan has argued, it is a critical concept for the future of work, and "anyone hoping to build a sustain-ing organisation in the 21st century needs to understand it" [9]. This chapter reframes organisational debt in relation to transformation (e.g. not reviewing structure, performance indicators, resourcing, etc.), and suggests tactics for paying back, and paying forward on the debt.

A second type of debt that we will introduce is that of the organ-isation's "sensemaking debt". The organisations that find it hardest to transform are often legacy enterprises rich in history, strong in identity, and steeped in organisational memory and knowledge. Organisational memory and knowledge are critical parts of how we frame and make sense of changing presents, and uncertain futures. In a transformation, these "memories" require purposeful updating and remaking in order to make them relevant for changing repertoires, and to re-code past experiences to orient them to the present and future. Human beings are "homo-prospectus" – we live our lives and make decisions with the future in mind, rather than merely optimis-ing to present conditions. We have a bias toward seeking meaning. Transformation therefore needs to carefully consider how the past can sit within the present and future, and provide a meaningful sen-semaking framework to support organisational evolvability that bal-ances the costs with outcomes.

Three sensemaking gaps are discussed in Chapter 4. In Chapter 4.1, we challenge traditional understanding of "scale", and call for a more nuanced and complex adaptive understanding of the con-cept. Traditional approaches to scale are shaped by a product-driven approach to scaling through replication. Replication is challenging when it comes to programs, ideas and design. Whilst pilots are useful for testing and refining ideas, these inevitably account for the pilot site's context. Pilots also tend to be "successful" as they enjoy extraor-dinary circumstances.

Scale works differently for complex adaptive systems, and here we introduce different ways of thinking about and approaching scale, as well as elaborate on their relevance with real world case studies. These approaches are as follows:

- Scaling out: Replicating or adapting programs/products to different contexts; but mindful where we need to replicate principles rather than the whole program.
- Scaling up: Managing formal systems and the constraints and conditions they create to enable ease of adoption.
- Scaling deep: Focusing on hearts and minds, influencing values, power distribution and relationships for long-term change.
- Scaling down: Recognising and allowing for local variations and adaptations.

In Chapter 4.2, we discuss the importance of actively facilitating collaborative sensemaking of change as a way to navigate the complexities of transformation, as well as to pay forward on organisational debt. Systems in transition inevitably occupy multiple possibilities and time trajectories of the change; even as we strive toward a vision of the future, we have to actively adapt existing practices to ensure we can keep the business going. The approaches we end up adopting throughout the journey often emerge from the active tension, and will also shift and adapt as we go along. Transformation efforts need to acknowledge, pay attention to, and actively manage these concurrent trajectories.

To illustrate these tensions, we introduce the Three-Horizons model from Bill Sharpe as a sensemaking framework that can help us to identify pathways that emerge from the different trajectories.

The horizons are:

- 1st Horizon (Visionary): Future-oriented, pockets of successful adaptation already exist.
- 2nd Horizon (Manager): Business-as-usual practices, "keeping the lights on" while phasing out obsolete elements.
- 3rd Horizon (Entrepreneur): Transitional practices integrating the future vision with present concerns.

Together, these three horizons intersect and allow a Triangle of Change to emerge. This triangle helps to map the space for experimentation and the potential pathways to change.

In Chapter 4.3, we highlight how organisations should be mindful of limitations when using metrics to measure complex systems like enterprises. We propose a different approach that factors in the need for a body of indicators: leading indicators, process indicators and outcome indicators in combination.

McKinsey has coined a new term that references their analytics around the metrics of transformation: "Transformatics" [10]. Their article discussing these Transformatics and the numbers behind successful transformations ends with an enigmatic statement that "the numbers tell the story". And, no doubt, numbers do tell a story. However, in the same vein, we are mindful that numbers can similarly belie many different stories and aspects of your transformation. Whilst measurement is good practice, we are mindful that measurement also perverts.

Relying solely on outcome-oriented metrics ignore the human aspect of change, and lead to unintended consequences and attribution errors. We illustrate this through a discussion of examples from modern history.

Leading indicators, such as changes in employee conversations, can provide early signals of how people are making sense of change and using it to guide their decisions and behaviour. These might then have impact on process indicators, such as the frequency of cross-silo interactions, and can help track how the change is being implemented. Outcome indicators, like customer satisfaction results remain important. However, we recognise that these tend to be lagging indicators that take time to show results, and that unintended outcomes might emerge from the interventions.

The chapter also emphasises the importance of qualitative data, such as employee stories and experiences, to understand the human side of change. Organisations should remember that people are complex and may not always respond predictably to change, even if the change is objectively beneficial.

We conclude in Chapter 5, with each co-author providing their perspective on enterprise transformation, and the importance of taking an approach which is focused on maintaining and enhancing the capacity of a system for adaptive evolution – evolvability.

Sunil discusses the need to move away from the traditional metamorphosis-driven approach of moving from one static state to another (like a caterpillar to a butterfly). Reprising the message that such an approach has created a 70% failure rate of transformation initiatives, he discusses key factors which are contributing to the failure of transformation initiatives.

He elaborates on how leadership can enable evolvability by reframing the role of leaders as orchestrators (rather than engineers) of change: Building the evolutionary capabilities of your organisation, being role models by walking the talk, adopting metrics that factor in the ability for responsive adaptation, and treating everyone in the enterprise as co-pilots, rather than passengers, in the evolutionary journey.

Sunil recognises the relevance of metamorphosis-driven transformation under specific circumstances, but advocates that a focus on building adaptive capability will allow organisations to be more responsive to change, and adapt in a manner that factors in their full potential. He concludes with a strong message that choosing a metamorphosis approach to transformation can threaten the survivability of an enterprise while those that choose evolution will not only survive, but thrive in a fast changing and disruptive environment.

Finally, Zhen concludes by providing clarification between the concepts of organisational evolution, and that of evolvability. Whilst the former focuses on the actual characteristics of change, and the processes which bring them about, evolvability looks at the system's ability and capacity to support on-going adaptive diversity in response to environmental pressures.

Whilst traditional planning tends to lead with visions of almost linear representations of change over time, the evolutionary biology from which we borrow the concept of evolvability indicate that change can take many different curves and forms. The real pathways of evolutionary change present more as a entangled web than a unidirectional curve. Recognising this means we need to reframe how we plan and enact change. Evolvability implies the need for multiple, ongoing experiments, as well as differentiated approaches that are nested in a disciplined way across different parts of the business.

Zhen concludes finally with the need to recognise that change is not an exceptional undertaking, nor a series of projects to complete. Continuous change is reality, transformation is the capability to live and thrive. For organisations to sustainably transform, we need to cultivate the capacity of their systems for regenerative adaptive diversity necessary to keep up with an ever-changing environment.

THEORY OF TRANSFORMATION

We are hard pressed, regardless of industry or sector, to find any-one who is not currently undergoing or contemplating some kind of transformation. We believe that this is a trend that will continue because transformation is not a "one-walk dog".

As we are faced with a complex world and entangled challenges, multidisciplinary, cross-sectoral learning and adaptation is becoming increasingly important as some challenges are so wicked that there is no way anyone can seek to solve them alone. Industry moves quickly as it is less encumbered by the complications that government and social sectors are under. As a result, government and social sectors have always been keen to learn from industry as they are better able to move and adapt quickly. However, as the world becomes aware of the realities of complexity, and embraces a more organic and humanistic approach to managing change, it might be useful for organisations to look across the fence into the social sectors who have always had to put humans and human systems at the heart of their transformation efforts.

Much of our organisational and sensemaking debt arises from the fact that our approaches to leading and managing transformation still begin with a mechanical metaphor of organisation: Believing we can implement transformation of human systems in a systematic and roadmapped way, and shepherd organisations from one stable state into another, with clear and measurable outcomes. But, humans systems are not machines, nor are people ants. They are organic, and people bring the extra complexity of not only behaving according to instinct. This mechanical metaphor has found its way into the social sector in the form of the prevalence of "theories of change".

To quote the United Nations Development Group's "Theory of Change companion", they define it as "a method that explains how a given intervention, or set of interventions, are expected to lead to a specific development change, drawing on a causal analysis based on available evidence" [11]. This language of linear causality, and inter-vention leading to desired change reflects back to us the way we have been getting transformation wrong. Problems such as poverty and climate change are wildly entangled in a world which is constantly buffeted by shifting tide winds. We intuit that such linear approaches will fall short. Here, we want to bring awareness to the need for embracing a more complex adaptive Theory of Transformation instead.

A theory of change specifies how a project or program attains desired outcomes. *Transformation is not a project.* It is multi-dimensional, multi-faceted, and multilevel, cutting across (boundaries) and intervention silos, across sectors and specialised interests, connecting local and global, and sustaining across time. A theory of transformation incorporates and integrates multiple theories of change operating at many levels that, knitted together, explain how major systems transformation occurs. [12]

It is with this, we invite you to journey with us on an approach to transformation that acknowledges the intersecting complexities of your organisation.

REFERENCES

[1]   Anne-Sylvanne Chassany. (16 Feb 2023) "CEOs forced to ditch decades of forecasting habits: Privately owned IKEA has shed the traditional budget to focus on scenario planning", in *Financial Times: Opinion - The Top Line.*

[2]   J.L. Bower & Clayton Christensen. (Jan–Feb 1995) "Disruptive technologies: Catching the wave", in *Harvard Business Review.*

[3]   "Disruption 2020: An Interview with Clayton Christensen". (Feb 2020) in *MIT Sloan Management Review*, Magazine Spring Issue. https://sloanreview.mit.edu/article/an-interview-with-clayton-m-christensen/

[4]   Lingfei Wu, Dashun Wang & James Evans. (2019) "Large teams develop and small teams disrupt science and technology", in *Nature* (566: 7744, 378–382).

[5]   Dider Bonnett. (Sept 2022) "3 stages of a successful digital transformation", in *Harvard Business Review.* https://hbr.org/2022/09/3-stages-of-a-successful-digital-transformation#:~:text=Most%20digital%20transformations%20fail.,with%20an%20average%20at%2087.5%25

[6]   Gerald Kane, Rich Nanda, Anh Nguyen Phillips & Jonathan Copulsky. (2023) *Transformation Myth: Leading your Organization through Uncertain Times.* The MIT Press.

[7]   C.M. Christensen. (Winter 1993) "The rigid disk-drive industry: A history of commercial and technological turbulence", in *Business History Review* (67: 4, 531–588).

[8]   Steve Blank. (May 2015) "Organizational debt is like technical debt – but worse", in *Forbes online.* https://www.forbes.com/sites/steveblank/2/?015/05/18/organizational-debt-is-like-technical-debt-but-worse-2/??sh=5fe686ac7b35

[9]   Aaron Dignan. (June 2016) "How to eliminate organisational debt", in *The Ready Blog.* Accessed 17 Jan 2023. https://medium.com/the-ready/how-to-eliminate-organizational-debt-8a949c06b61b

[10]   McKinsey Quarterly. (Oct 2019) "The numbers behind successful transformations". Accessed 17 Jan 2023. https://www.mckinsey.com/capabilities/transformation/our-insights/the-numbers-behind-successful-transformations

[11]   United Nations Development Group. (2017) *Theory of Change: UNDAP Companion Guidance*. Accessed 17 Jan 2023. https://unsdg.un.org/sites/default/files/UNDG-UNDAF-Companion-Pieces-7-Theory-of-Change.pdf

[12]   Blue Marble Evaluation. "Theory of transformation principle". Accessed 17 Jan 2023. https://bluemarbleeval.org/principles/operating-principles/theory-transformation-principle

One

INTRODUCTION

A leading bank in Asia had a goal of becoming more customer-centric. As a part of its digital transformation efforts, it began by transforming its IT functions. The bank wanted to improve its innovation cycle and product development lead times. Its goal was to improve the lead time that a product idea spent in IT. The transformation effort was declared a success because they had managed to reduce the time a product idea spent in IT from 5 to 3 months – nearly halving the time! However, clients were still working with legacy products long after the new products had left IT. Management was wondering where the successes of their transformation could be seen. The overall lead time for turning a product idea into an offering, and delivering it into the hands of its customers was 21 months. The time spent in IT had been reduced from 5 to 3 months. The rest of the 18 months were spent upstream making its convoluted way across business prioritisation, budgeting and capacity allocation.

Across the ocean, a large military outfit was looking to transform itself by upgrading its technology systems. They spent $5 billion dollars over 8 years to try to overhaul their old systems and move toward an integrated system to enhance better workflow. The post-mortem of this failure cited it as a good example of an "organisational failure". A direct quote from the report stated that

> as the project team continued through the implementation journey, key stakeholders and employees strongly resisted changes to future business processes and the capabilities… The team clearly struggled to overcome the highly tenured employees, bureaucracy and inflexible operations and failed to implement many of the changes as a result.

The transformation was divorced from the organisational realities of its implementation – that we needed to bring the people along with us, and be flexible to change. The transformation plan needs to evolve

DOI: 10.4324/9781003505433-2

alongside updating business processes, on-going capacity building and operational adjustments [1].

These are two very different examples – across different levels of scale, types of organisation and extent of impact. Those who are working in the space of affecting change and bringing about transformation, however, will likely find much resonance in the circumstances described. Transformation in both cases was too focused on patchwork approaches, rather than adopting a systems view. Parts of the enterprise will drag its feet as it is unaligned with the new ways of working, especially when transformation leads fall for a "technology fallacy" and do not recognise that all transformation – digital or otherwise – is "primarily about people and... involves changes to organisational dynamics and how work gets done. A focus only on selecting and implementing the right digital technologies is not likely to lead to success" [2].

"Changing the culture" has become a buzz-phrase for those working in organisational transformation. Organisations are all seeking ways to change "the company culture to be more agile, risk tolerant, and experimental" [2]. However, whilst culture is a universal truth, it is also individually unique to every organisation, and defies simple measures. The culture has to evolve alongside the transformation; however, transformation initiatives are often undertaken with the intent to move the needle on the outcomes in areas that are business related. The success of transformation is often also linked to proxy metrics which are:

- Business related – Some examples include increasing revenue, profit or market share.
- Customer related – Some examples include improving customer satisfaction and customer retention.
- Product related – Some examples include quicker time to market, and improving the quality of product and services.
- Employee related – Some examples include enhancing employee engagement and talent acquisition.
- Technology related – Some examples include progressing on digital maturity, or modernising legacy system.

Oftentimes, there will be some positive impact experienced when transformation efforts first get underway. For example, where Agile and Lean transformations often lead with a focus on people and process. Despite some teething pains, organisations will often benefit from better visualisation of workflow, thereby developing a better under-standing of dependencies and blockers. This creates an awareness of a need for better cross-functional collaboration across teams and func-tions. Technology-led transformations tend to lead to improved collab-oration between technology and business functions. There are green shoots that are created by the initial interventions. However, these also tend to stop short as the framing of transformations tend to be about "moving the needle on specific outcomes", and the efforts stop evolving once organisations declare success or failure on those metrics. Whilst it is understandable that metrics provide useful guide posts, they can also lead to tunnel vision.

When these green shoots run into the constraints of culture and structure (formal and informal), which are harder to shift, transforma-tions tend to lose steam as they are overly focused on evolution across phases, rather than focusing on developing the organisation's abil-ity to evolve; or its "evolvability". Transformation requires on-going adaptability even against challenges like structural silos, hierarchical power structures, annual big bang budgeting and ossified performance appraisals that often slow down the momentum that early transforma-tion efforts bring.

OFFERING AN ALTERNATE FRAME TO MAKE SENSE OF TRANSFORMATION

In this book, we wish to offer an alternate frame to leaders, manag-ers and anyone who has agency to affect change within their system. In the past 10 years, we have witnessed a distinct shift in the meta-phors of organisation [3, 4], from presenting them as stable mecha-nistic systems in homeostasis, to organisations as living ecosystems, enmeshed within even broader ecosystems of competitors, supply chains, customers, partners and constellations of unknown and unknowable network effects. The concept of organisational evolu-tion borrows concepts and thinking from evolutionary biology, and whilst there is recognition now that competition and shifting envi-ronmental factors create a need for consistent evolution, the popular frames of transformation still present as moves from one static state to another preferred state of homeostasis.

The familiar approach to planning and implementing a transfor-mation journey would be to understand where you are, determine some preferred strategic outcome you would like to achieve and then identify how you will get there. This appears like a sound approach to journey and project planning, and there is nothing wrong with the basic thinking. However, change journeys often take place over time, where the already turbulent seas we are navigating present new challenges and surprises along the way. The organisations which struggle the most with change and transformation also tend to be mature enterprises who have achieved levels of success with existing models, practices and strategies: "Why rock the boat?" is the common thinking. Organisational inertia strengthens with success, and it is already hard to turn the boat in rough seas. It is harder still when parts of your system are committed to a previous pattern, and working against you. Can you sail to a predetermined destination in rough seas, a shifting landscape, potential unknown sea monsters (read industry disruptors) who appear out of nowhere, and a divided crew?

The frame we would like to offer instead is to begin with the understanding that we are not working with a static system. At the expense of being trite, we suffer the unique curse of "living in interesting times". There is at each individual level, an appreciation for the complexities and uncertainties that every day presents. However, when we start to fractally shift from a personal level of reflection to the organisational level, we seem to abandon this intuitive understanding, and assume stability as the norm. Most organisations are remarkably slow to transform because people tend to crave familiarity − what we know, and are used to, are comforting. Prof. Nathan Furr from INSEAD, who studies innovation, strategy and uncertainty, refers to this as our tendency to seek out "uncertainty balancers". The more uncertain things are, the more we seek out and reinforce the comfortable [5]. Leadership coaches Jennifer Garvey Berger and Carolyn Coughlin elaborate further on this by explaining a "complexity paradox" [6]. Human beings, they explain, have a natural inclination toward complexity and handling uncertainty. However, when there is too much uncertainty and ambiguity, our ability to tap into this capability becomes compromised.

TRANSFORMATION AS EVOLUTION: ORGANISING TO GUIDE BECOMING

Transformation needs to be regarded as a part of on-going change and evolution, and recognise that we are working with a complex human system, embedded within broader emergent systems. Each journey is therefore unique to every organisation, and will require recognising a need for consistent adaptation in the selected approaches and tactics. Strategically designing and implementing transformation requires an approach that has consistent feedback loops, and responsive review cycles. Plans need to recognise the organisation as a living and morphing system that is consistently in a state of "becoming". The transformation will likely be negotiated across different levels – corporate, business model and day-to-day – and different areas of the living system in independent and diverse ways. Effective transformation efforts focus on allowing healthy variation and distributed sense-making of change within a strategically aligned direction. That is, we allow for the organisation to navigate and negotiate its ongoing "becoming". We recognise that a uniform, neat and episodic transformation is inorganic and impractical.

Here we draw on the work of Karl Weick, an American organisational theorist, who has contributed to developing the field of organisational sensemaking. One of the most significant contributions that Weick has made to the field of management science, is shifting the focus of "organisation", to that of "organising" instead [7]. In doing so, he highlights the on-going process-oriented aspect of organisational activities. Rather than moving from one stable state to another discrete point, change is consistently unfolding and experienced by practitioners as an emergent "flow of possibilities, and a conjunction of events and open-ended interactions occurring over time" [8]. In this view, the act of transforming is part of an on-going evolution.

ORGANISATIONAL EVOLUTION AND THE RED QUEEN EFFECT

Organisational evolution theory can be classified broadly into three main threads. The first focuses on situating organisational phases of maturity into corporate life cycles. Owners or managers of businesses often speak of being at "this stage of business" or of "needing something to move the business to the next level" [9]. For example, popular models like Adizes Corporate Life Cycle or the Greiner Growth Model [10] help us to understand how corporations move from one stage to another, and to identify and overcome challenges faced by each stage from start-up, to growth and stability. It also warns of the inertia that success breeds, entrenching bureaucracy that leads to potential decline and death if the corporation gets stuck in its own success trap.

Organisations seeking transformation typically find themselves in some kind of bureaucratic bind, where the ecosystem presents a shifting landscape and new pressures, and organisational renewal through transformation is necessary for its ongoing survival and sustainability. The revolutionary ideas that helped organisations to evolve from one stage of maturity to another become inapplicable to a different phase, and new revolutionary ideas and patterns need to come in.

The second thread in organisational evolution literature draws heavily upon Darwinian concepts of on-going competition for fitness. These borrow from the science behind genetic selection (variation, selection and retention of traits based on fitness). The Red Queen effect in organisational learning explains this nicely:

> An organisation facing competition is likely to engage in a search for ways to improve performance. When successful, this search results in learning that is likely to increase the organisation's competitive strength, which in turn triggers learning in its rivals consequently making them stronger competitors and so again triggering learning in the first organisation... the conditions under which this self-reinforcing process, known in evolutionary theory as the 'Red Queen'. [11]

The Red Queen makes reference to the Lewis Carroll classic, *Alice in Wonderland*, where Alice meets the Red Queen who is always running just to stay in the same place. That is, responding to competition alone is not sufficient as the self-reinforcing nature of market learning means that the smarter you get, the smarter your competitors; and vice versa. Survival requires us to co-evolve with the systems we interact with, and our evolutionary trajectories need to be ever adaptive to smartly transform. Darwin noted that whilst animals all co-evolve in response to each other, the fact that some do go extinct, and some adapt better to shifting environments, implies that not all of them evolve at the same rate. For example, in North America, the vanishing wolf packs have been attributed to shrinking forests and decreasing hunting ground and food supply. Whilst wolves are on the list of endangered species, coyotes have thrived and are frequently sighted in cities. Coyotes are able to thrive in urban environments because they managed to adapt to take advantage of small ranges of habitat, and also became less picky about what they ate. This created an adaptive advantage that has helped them to thrive despite facing the same environmental conditions as their canine cousin.

One of the most often quoted (and mis-quoted) phrases from Charles Darwin's work on evolution is "survival of the fittest". This has often been interpreted to place focus on survival through natural selection of genetic traits that are "fit" because they bring competitiveness. However, modern evolutionary biology has shed light on the deeper meaning, and more important aspect of the phrase, which is the focus on the reproduction of genetic mutation and variation. Accelerated evolution and transformation in species and the rise of dominant species have also been proven by biologists to be more likely caused by opportunistic moves into new ecological niches, rather than through mere competition alone [12, 13].

With its success, it is unlikely that we consider health and organic good business, Whole Foods, as a niche business. However, that was actually where it began. It specifically targeted a niche of affluent, conscious consumers who place a premium on their health and wellness, rather than competing purely on price and wide distribution of stores. They recognised that not everyone would want, or be able to spend a premium on groceries. Whole Foods focused on organic foods before you could find organics everywhere, and the buzz continues. It spawned a new competitive niche of organic food groups which did not exist before. They built a brand around specific customers who value quality. Amazon has since acquired Whole Foods, and one of the main reasons they cited for their acquisition was to access their customers, in part because of their loyalty and buying power.

When we conduct a deeper exploration of this metaphor, what becomes apparent is that the responsiveness and the ability to adapt are more critical than mere enhancement of competitiveness. With our canine friends, it was coyotes understanding how to live in increasingly urban environments. With businesses, it is about identifying adjacent spaces the business can thrive and maintain its core purpose in. Or, in the words of Darwin: "It is not the strongest of the species that survives, nor the most intelligent, but the one most responsive to change".

FOCUS ON EVOLVABILITY; NOT EVOLUTION

This brings us to the third theme that emerges in the literature on organisational evolution: That genuine organisational evolution is actually a continuous complex adaptive process that emerges through enhancing the adaptability of the system – and distributing response-ability to its talent force. Transformation occurs not through a backroom strategy devised by master strategists (read: senior leadership) being rolled out, but through localised decisions and actions taken in day-to-day organisational operations and activities. Transformation strategies are often first imagined as grand strategic changes, as the effort requires visioning. However, it is in the day-to-day tactical response, implementation and monitoring of the efforts that it becomes clear that transformation is a process of making, as well as responding and adjusting to change. These micro-decisions and actions are what collectively form the assemblage that presents itself as observable change.

We go back now to the example of how the humble coyote was able to thrive while its more noble and dominant alpha cousin, the wolf, dwindled. To bridge this example back to industry, one 1975 Harvard Business Review magazine article declared that organisations should seek to increase "Market Share (as) a Key to profitability". In this article, the authors explored the positive correlation between market share and ROI citing known benefits such as economies of scale, market power, and quality of management as factors that directly drive the positive correlation between [14]. However, we fast-forward close to 50 years to 2021, and the HBR is citing "Adaptability (as) The New Competitive Advantage" due to the increasingly uncertain conditions that organisations now compete under.

Traditional approaches to strategy assume that the world is relatively stable and predictable. But globalisation, new technologies, and greater transparency have combined to upend the business environment. In this period of risk and uncertainty, more and more managers are finding competitive advantage in organisational capabilities that foster rapid adaptation. Instead of being really good at doing some particular thing, companies must be really good at learning how to do new things.

Those that thrive are quick to read and act on weak signals of change. They have worked out how to experiment rapidly and frequently not only with products and services but also with business models, processes, and strategies. They have acquired the skills to manage complex multi stakeholder systems in an increasingly interconnected world.

And, perhaps most important, they have learned to unlock their greatest resource: the people who work for them.

The once strong correlation between profitability and industry share is now almost nonexistent in some sectors. According to research from the Boston Consulting Group, the probability that the market share leader is also the profitability leader declined from 34% in 1950 to just 7% in 2007 [15]. Strategy now is, therefore, a more complex endeavour than merely seeking to become a market leader. In many cases, being a more agile player allows adaptability and manoeuvrability that being a market leader does not. Companies from digital-first players like Google, to legacy organisations like GE have embraced complex multi-company systems of smaller companies as they have recognised that it reduces their constraints, and creates a better ecosystem of smaller and interdependent systems for ongoing experimentation and transformation, rather than relying on single-player dominance.

Nokia is a famous example of a once dominant player that got outstripped by competitors like Apple and Google who recognised that it would be better to harness and mobilise the complex and interdependent web of hardware and application partners rather than seek to be the dominant market leader. Stephen Elop, Nokia's CEO, famously wrote in a memo to his staff, "Our competitors aren't taking our market share with devices; they are taking our market share with an entire ecosystem."

Elop's internal memo to his staff has been released to the public, and we share extracts from it below, as his description of the market re-organisation and complexification that from 2011 marked just the early signs of a world that has grown even more entangled and complex.

> I have learned that we are standing on a burning platform. And, we have more than one explosion - we have multiple points of scorching heat that are fuelling a blazing fire around us.
>
> For example, there is intense heat coming from our competitors, more rapidly than we ever expected. Apple disrupted the market by redefining the smartphone and attracting developers to a closed, but very powerful ecosystem....

At the lower-end price range, Chinese OEMs are cranking out a device much faster than, as one Nokia employee said only partially in jest, "the time that it takes us to polish a PowerPoint presentation." They are fast, they are cheap, and they are challenging us.

And the truly perplexing aspect is that we're not even fighting with the right weapons. We are still too often trying to approach each price range on a device-to-device basis.

The battle of devices has now become a war of ecosystems, where ecosystems include not only the hardware and software of the device, but developers, applications, ecommerce, advertising, search, social applications, location-based services, unified communications and many other things. Our competitors aren't taking our market share with devices; they are taking our market share with an entire ecosystem. This means we're going to have to decide how we either build, catalyse or join an ecosystem.

How did we get to this point? Why did we fall behind when the world around us evolved?

This is what I have been trying to understand. I believe at least some of it has been due to our attitude inside Nokia. We poured gasoline on our own burning platform. I believe we have lacked accountability and leadership to align and direct the company through these disruptive times. We had a series of misses. We haven't been delivering innovation fast enough. We're not collaborating internally. [16]

As Elop described, a pure review of competitors showed that they had been outstripped not at a Red Queen level "I will match you bet-for-bet" approach, but through the rapid mutation. The market had moved away from the device-centred platforms that Nokia had been used to, into that of smartphone ecosystems which integrated developers, applications, ecommerce, advertising, search, social applications, location-based services, unified communications into a single environment. They were no longer competing in the same way they had been used to imagining.

These days, we are facing environments where such smart integration has gone beyond platforms, and into the vertical integration of supply chains for truly just-in-time production, and truly customised products and services. In our book, we will be discussing this through the innovative RenDanHeYi organisation made famous by Haier's organisational design and business results. Translated, it refers to the integration of employers in an organisation with the needs or demand of users, facilitated by a distributed team-of-teams or micro-enterprise design (Chapter 3).

We now understand that people seek personal growth and meaning in their work, and the ability to understand the impact they make, as well as how they are connected to a bigger purpose and network. Organisational transformation that matters, therefore, rests on the ability of management to more effectively mobilise people – employees, suppliers, cross-industry partners and independent developers and players – as well as cultivate a system that allows for continuous adaptability. Agility achieved through effective distribution of the right levels of decision-making, leadership, experimentation and autonomy throughout the organisation, whilst maintaining the right feedback loops in the system help organisations to achieve a metabolism that provides the right balance between empowered adaptation across different levels and parts of the organisation, as well as coordination that can steer broader transformation in a coherent manner. Contrary to classical strategic thinking and planning where the organisation follows strategy, this age of uncertainty means that transformation requires strategy to follow the organising instead.

Short and effective feedback loops need to be put in place to coordinate continuous sensing, adapting and corresponding responses. Transformation is about capabilities and conditions, rather than merely outcomes. We enhance organisational *evolvability*, rather than fixate on moving from one stage of evolution to another.

TRANSFORMING FOR EVOLVABILITY – A REFRAME

Effective transformation is an ongoing effort at enhancing an organisation's evolve-ability, and response-ability. The efforts help the enterprise to distribute the ability to respond to change, and maintain direction and alignment without losing its adaptability. In this section, we review some of the common challenges that transformation efforts face and suggest a simple re-framing to support enhancing evolvability.

Monitor health; not just shifting the needle on transformation goals
It is extremely rare to come across a transformation program that explicitly has an objective of enhancing enterprise agility, health

and overall evolvability. Often specific measures are set to measure improvements of the business impact; however, monitoring organisational health, adaptability and agility are neglected, or included as ill-fitting afterthoughts.

On top of watching how the needle shifts on business impact, we recommend designing transformation with an eye on monitoring on-going organisational health as well. Include adaptability and agility (not Agile!) measures. For example, monitoring decision cycle times as a way to measure organisational capacity for quick response. Beyond efficiency of cycle times, timely reviews and debriefs should also be conducted to understand where improvements can be made, as well as how the situation has evolved that might require a different benchmark to be set for *effective* decision cycle times.

Bridge the System and Local Optimisation

At the beginning of this chapter, we cited two very different examples of digital transformation efforts, which suffered from the same issues. Most enterprises we have encountered are investing, or contemplating some form of investment in technology to elevate their game. It is widely recognised now that IT should not merely be treated as a cost centre, but as a strategic business function [17]. The right technology improves customer offerings and experience and also increases the speed of response to changes in the external environment. The realisation that technology is a key differentiator has led this wave of Digital or IT transformation.

This IT focus often brings some benefits. Leaders looking just to "shift the needle" tend to be content in the beginning with these early wins. This combined with the incentive to declare their transformation as a success, has led to interventions being limited to the IT function only. The lack of a systems-level view often results in broader systems-level constraints not getting addressed.

Local optimisation that is uncoordinated leads to friction when inevitable inertia in the rest of the enterprise emerges. This inertia, rooted in the traditional ways of working and legacy organisational culture, is far stronger a force than any momentum created by localised interventions. There needs to be purposeful and intentional coordination of efforts to connect local optimisation across the organisation, as well as to bridge and integrate these effects to the systems level. You need a combination of smaller and concentrated teams and also not neglect the team-of-teams that will be required to create systems-level transformation [18].

Cultivate Learning and Innovation alongside Transformation

The transformation journey for each organisation will be unique. Whilst there are generic lessons that can be learnt across cases, the actual journey is a path that is made by walking. The lack of directly transferable best practices means that organisations will have to run multiple experiments to learn what works best for their unique enterprise. Experiments, by definition, are designed to test ideas and hypotheses that are not sure about. The experiment is a data-gathering exercise. It might not "yield the intended outcomes" immediately. As a result, without the right attitude, experiments often get dismissed as "failures" rather than learning experiences. For decades, enterprises were modelled like machines, to optimise on predictability, certainty and stability. Experimentation was considered something that was to be avoided and mitigated, and innovation limited to the Research and Development department. This leads to taking comfort in the status quo and avoiding taking ownership of change, let alone initiating it. However, if we are seeking organisational evolvability we are also seeking the same genetic variability that helps some species to thrive over others. Experimentation allows us to test variability to understand the ones that will work for us.

Transformation is also a messy and non-linear journey. There must be space for emergence and unintended consequences of the interventions. Typically transformation plans are underestimated, and tied to a tight timeline. This often results in change being pushed despite there being no appetite for change. It also means disregarding valuable learning opportunities. Organisations that are able to develop a culture of learning from on-going experimentation are better disposed to evolvability. The unintended consequences also mean that there could be valuable opportunities for beneficial mutation in the enterprise's DNA. Transformation will present opportunities for innovation. The post-Covid world we live in has turned many organisations around to the innovation value that can come from crisis [19, 20]; however, transformation also presents an experimental space that lends itself well to innovation. Organisations that can develop a culture of learning and actively deploy innovation alongside the learning experiences that transformation experiences will provide will also benefit.

In Chapter 2, we will review multiple types and forms of organisational transformations to discuss archetypes of transformation and provide typological dimensions that can help transformation agents to make sense of their own journeys.

REFERENCES

[1] United States Senate. (July 2014) "The air force's Expeditionary Combat Support System (ECSS): A cautionary tale on the need for business process reengineering and complying with acquisition best practices". Accessed 25 Jan 2023. https://www.hsgac.senate.gov/wp-content/uploads/imo/media/doc/PSI%20REPORT%20-%20The%20Air%20Force's%20ECSS%20(July%207%202014).pdf

[2] Gerald C. Kane, Anh Nguyen Phillips, Jonathan R. Copulsky & Garth R. Andrus. (2022) The Technology Fallacy: How People are the Real Key to Digital Transformation. MIT Press.

[3] Gareth Morgan. (2011) "Reflections on images of organization and its implications for organization and environment", in Organization & Environment (24: 4, 459–478). https://doi.org/10.1177/1086026611434274

[4] Gareth Morgan. (1986) Images of Organization. Sage Publications.

[5] Nathan Furr. (27 March 2020) "You're not powerless in the face of uncertainty", in Harvard Business Review. https://hbr.org/2020/03/youre-not-powerless-in-the-face-of-uncertainty

[6] Jennifer Garvey-Berger & Carolyn Coughlin. (2022) Unleash your Complexity Genius: Growing Your Inner Capacity to Lead. Stanford University Press.

[7] Karl Weick. (1979) The Social Psychology of Organizing, 2nd ed. Addison-Wesley.

[8] Haridimos Tsoukas & Robert Chia. (2002) "On organizational becoming: Rethinking organizational change", in Organization Science (13: 5, 567–582).

[9] Robert Phelps, Richard Adams & John Bessant. (2007) "Life cycles of growing organizations: A review with implications for knowledge and learning", in International Journal of Management Reviews (9: 1, 1–30).

[10] Larry Greiner. (1972, republished again in 1998) "Evolution and Revolution as Organizations Grow", in Harvard Business Review.

[11] William Barnett & Morten Hansen. (1996) "The red queen in organizational evolution", in Strategic Management Journal (17, 139–157).

[12] Momme von Sydow. (2014) "Survival of the fittest in Darwinian metaphysics - Tautology or Testable Theory?", in E. Voigts, B. Schaff & M. Piertrzak-Franger (eds.) Reflecting on Darwin. Ashgate.

[13] Sarda Sahney, Michael J. Benton & Paul A. Ferry. (2010) "Links between global taxonomic diversity, ecological diversity and expansion of vertebrates on land", in *Biology Letters* (6: 4, 544–547).

[14] Robert D. Buzzell, Bradley T. Gale & Ralph Sultan. (June 1975) "Market share - A key to profitability", in *Harvard Business Review Magazine*. https://hbr.org/1975/01/market-share-a-key-to-profitability

[15] Martin Reeves & Mike Deimler. (July/August 2011) "Adaptability: The new competitive advantage", in *Harvard Business Review Magazine*.

[16] Charles Arthur. "Nokia's chief executive to staff: 'We are standing on a burning platform'", in *The Guardian, Technology Blog*. Accessed 3 Nov 2023. https://www.theguardian.com/technology/blog/2011/feb/09/nokia-burning-platform-memo-elop

[17] Sunil Mundra. "The behavioural implications of treating your IT function as a cost centre", in *Thoughtworks Insight*. Accessed 30 Jan 2023. https://www.thoughtworks.com/en-sg/insights/blog/digital-transformation/behavioral-implications-treating-IT-as-cost-center-part-2

[18] Gen. Stanley McChrystal, Tantum Collins, David Silverman & Chris Fussell. (2015) *Team of Teams: New Rules of Engagement for a Complex World*. Portfolio/Penguin.

[19] Jordan Bar Am, Laura Furstenthal, Felicitas Jorge & Erik Roth. (June 17, 2020) "Innovation in a crisis: Why is it more critical than ever?", in *Mckinsey & Company Articles*. Accessed 30 Jan 2023. https://www.mckinsey.com/capabilities/strategy-and-corporate-finance/our-insights/innovation-in-a-crisis-why-it-is-more-critical-than-ever

[20] Microsoft Stories Asia. (10 Sept 2020) "When a crisis becomes an opportunity: A culture of innovation fuels business resilience and economic recovery". Accessed 30 Jan 2023. https://news.microsoft.com/apac/features/when-crisis-becomes-an-opportunity/

Two

INTRODUCTION

One of the things that defines us as humans is our propensity for stories. We love to tell them, to hear them, and to have them carry the answers to some of our most important and bewildering questions. We love them so much that we string together stories with a sort of once-upon-a-time feel about just about everything, with one thing leading naturally to the next. Looking back at something, we can tell a coherent story about it that makes it sound inevitable and neat. This is all beautiful—we even teach leaders to do this so that they can capture the hearts and minds of the people they lead. But it's not without its challenges. The problem is twofold. First, we try to use that same skill looking forward (which in complexity you can't, because you can't tell which of the many, many possibilities will emerge until after it has emerged). Second, in reality the story wasn't that clean or inevitable in the first place. We made it simple in our memory looking back and now we imagine an equally simple plot line going forward. [1]

Organisational change and transformation are intensive efforts. They require organisational commitment to resources, new goals and ways of working that often result in discomfort and disruption, and short-term opportunity costs. Careful time and effort are often invested in planning and creating some form of a roadmap for the journey. Folded into the roadmap are objectives and guidelines that are meant to discipline the effort. These objectives also help to articulate outcomes, goals and targets that can be used to signify and herald a "successful transformation". Whilst a lot of intense and intelligent thinking and analysis goes into such endeavours, transformations often deviate from the roadmap as envisioned. All change has consequences, and the unintended consequences will often outnumber the intended ones. The organisation is not a closed system, it is subject to influences

DOI: 10.4324/9781003505433-3

from a volatile world. Plans made at a specific point in time, are incapable of factoring in emergence and all its potential possibilities. The roadmap is a simple story that limits how we scan and plan.

Leadership expert Jennifer Garvey Berger, who helps organisations to cultivate leaders who are better equipped to face complexity, calls this simple story one of the key mind traps we tend to fall into. We seek simple beginnings, middles and ends, and fill in missing pieces according to the narrative we believe [2]. Whilst these work in systems that are closed or highly ordered, an organisation is a complex ecosystem that is both open, emergent and consistently self-organising. We have to plan ahead for transformation moves such as large structural reorganisation. However, we must also appreciate the need for adaptability, and to constantly revisit and review our plans. As we have also covered in Chapter 1, there is often also not a clear "end" to our transformation stories, particularly when the focus is on enhancing on-going evolvability.

BETWEEN PLANNED CHANGE AND EMERGENT CHANGE

A roadmap approach is a "planned change" initiative. Planned change is usually an intentional and top-management initiative. The process tends to be guided by what is assumed to be linear and well-defined stages, and the thinking and process are governed by rationality and determinism [3–5]. The father of planned change management is theorist, researcher and practitioner in interpersonal and intergroup relationships, Kurth Lewin. Lewin proposed that before change and new behaviour can be adopted successfully, previous behaviour has to be disrupted and discarded. He suggested that change involves three steps or semi-stable stages that balance inhibiting and enabling environmental forces that call for change. The first stage is "unfreezing", where unhelpful behaviour needs to be made explicit and concrete change enacted to discard the behaviours that have been identified. The next stage is "moving", where through trial-and-error and research-based action the change slowly gets implemented. Once a suitable change is identified and implemented, the "refreezing" stage begins to embed the new changes in a state of quasi-equilibrium so they are learned and assimilated enough to be maintained in the future.

This model of change acknowledges the behavioural science of human systems, structures, processes and culture that need to co-evolve to support the successful adoption of new approaches. The general principle is sound, however, it makes some critical assumptions that create a simple story that belies the messy reality of change. The belief that a system can be frozen and unfrozen at specific levels makes a base assumption that organisations are closed and ordered systems, where any change implemented will evolve only within the framework of the imagined future. This approach has been criticised for ignoring environmental factors that are inconsistent with planned change initiatives. It presents organisational change as occurring in static phases, not dynamic interrelatedness and complexity [6]. Today, changes around the organisation are also taking place at such speed that it is nearly impossible to fully align behaviours to a static framework, and still respond to these pressures.

Emeritus Professor of Change and Leadership at Harvard Business Review, John Kotter [7], identified eight key reasons why planned change initiatives tend to experience failure. These are as follows: (1) failure to establish adequate urgency to change; (2) an insufficiently powerful guiding coalition; (3) lacking a vision; (4) under-communicating the vision (by up to a factor of ten); (5) not removing obstacles to the new vision; (6) failure to create systematic short term wins; and most critically, the final two reasons were (7) declaring victory too soon; and (8) not anchoring changes in the corporation's culture. Kotter's main thesis is that real change needs to run deep, and whereas declaring wins are important, they simply signify the beginning of change. Deeper steps need to be undertaken, particularly in an increasingly complex and uncertain world, where the demands are constantly shifting, and change is no longer a destination, but a way of being [8].

The plot twist in most simple stories of planned change tends to come from emergent change. Whereas planned change takes an episodic model to change (unfreeze-move-refreeze; changing from one state to another) and assumes we move from one state of equilibrium to another, emergent change embraces a more processual model, and sits in the school of organisational becoming [4]. Emergent change is all the stuff that happens because of the unintended consequences and unpredictability endemic to complex systems — "one must allow for emergence and surprise, meaning that one must take into account the possibility of organisational change having ramifications and implications beyond those initially imagined or planned" [9].

Emergent change is often a result of the informal self-organisation of agents within a system. Wanda Orlikowski of the MIT School of Management suggested in her seminal work on transformation that organisational change programmes need to be *made to work*, and that transformation only happens through a process of ongoing improvisation by agents in the system. They only "work" insofar as they are fine-tuned and adjusted by actors in particular contexts – and they are further changed on an ongoing basis to meet new realities [10]. Think, "Hey guys, this is what the higher-ups want, let's find a way to make it work", or "This keeps happening, let's find a way to make things work with this new reality". Change emerges as people interpret and organise work, and strive to improve the enabling conditions of their environment to support specific patterns. This is an on-going iterative process.

This version of change also challenges the basic notion that organisations operate in a state of static equilibrium. With the consistent instability and change in our environment, Complexity thinker, Ralph Stacey, suggests that organisations more likely than not operate at the "edge of chaos and far-from-equilibrium" [11]. To stay relevant and viable, organisations need to learn to operate with both stability and instability, since too much stability and control will cause the organisation to become unresponsive to its environment and decline, and no stability leads to too much stress and a lack of process [12]. Change is therefore continuous and emergent, and is responsive to the environment and ongoing learning.

Or, as Karl Weick puts more eloquently:

Sensitivity to local contingencies; suitability for on-line real-time experimentation, learning and sense-making, comprehensibility and manageability; likelihood of satisfying needs of autonomy, control, and expression; proneness to swift implementation, resistance to unravelling; ability to exploit existing tacit knowledge; and tightened and shortened feedback loops from results to action. [13]

ORGANISATIONAL TRANSFORMATION IN COMPLEX ADAPTIVE ORGANISATIONS

Whilst we have covered the differences between planned and emergent change, transformation journeys are not purely one or the other, and will require us to both plan, as well as allow for change to emerge. Traditional management has been based on machine and engineering-based metaphors of closed systems, where we can design and manipulate simple input and outputs to a system, and engineer for planned change and greater efficiencies. This has enabled many systems to stabilise and grow. In this version of reality, everything can be known, agreed and solved. However, in response to the volatility, uncertainty, complexity and ambiguity that real-world living and compound environmental effects present, management literature has evolved rapidly from this assumption.

Particularly in the past few years where we navigated COVID-19, and its after-effects, we have been presented with patterns we have never seen or experienced before, and where our traditional ways of knowing, planning and acting are poor responses. Disruptions have spanned from supply chain disruptions, to shifting employee value systems and more. The organisation as a system is not as bounded as we had previously imagined – we cannot define simple inputs and outputs, and sub-systems the way that general systems theory has suggested. Everything is so entangled and interdependent now that we cannot change one thing, and not expect for the rest of the system to also experience consequences.

UNDERSTANDING COMPLEXITY

The basic distinction between traditional approaches and complexity-based approaches have been presented as a distinction between Complicated systems and Complex systems. Paul Cilliers, who was one of the world's foremost thinkers of Complexity, famously uses this following analogy, "a jumbo jet is complicated but a mayonnaise is complex". As sophisticated and amazing as a jumbo jet is, it is a closed system that is equal to the sum of its parts. Mayonnaise, however, is complex because once you have mixed the ingredients in, you are no longer able to decide you really needed that last egg yolk for an omelette, and to separate the parts out of the mayonnaise. There is an irreversibility to the action, and the parts become fundamentally changed by the interaction. When looking at complexity, therefore, we need to look at rich interconnectivity and interrelations, and we focus on the relationships and interactions between parts of the system.

UNDERSTANDING COMPLEX ADAPTIVE SYSTEMS

Complex Adaptive Systems (CAS) is a combination of complexity, and recognising organisations as learning, adaptive and self-organising systems. Here, the agents in the system can self-organise and adapt to changing conditions both internal and external to the system. Start-ups and start-up culture are often referenced when describing systems that are open and responsive to environmental change. These companies tend to be very smart at self-organising, improvising and innovating in their utilisation of (what are often limited) resources (whether its information, energy, material and capital) to deliver value to customers. They also shift and develop new structures as they grow and expand into new markets [14]. These companies, however, tend to struggle with developing more stable and complicated systems as they grow. Their culture and behavioural patterns have been based on on-going and radical improvisation and self-organisation.

Whereas start-ups struggle to instil discipline to shift into more stable complicated systems, established companies often struggle in the other direction. They have gotten so successful at an existing business model and have optimised their operating model to exploit an existing pattern of success that they find it hard to be responsive to new patterns that challenge what they have become used to. Whilst all human systems are complex, enterprises display greater variability in their abilities to be adaptive and responsive based on their cultures and organisational design, and tend to cycle between periods of higher stability and instability.

As a result, planned change provides us with a guideline, but organisations are not static systems that can have change done to them. They learn and respond, and might surprise us with unintended consequences.

When these principles are applied across organisations and human systems, complicated systems are able to develop standardised industry good practice. The heavy repeatability and predictability also allow for governing rules to be developed. In complex systems, however, the constant emergence through self-organisation means we have to be open to shifting our approaches as the context changes and new patterns emerge. Attempts to apply artificial control in complex adaptive systems are what cause it to become unhealthy; just as the removal of wolves through human intervention did to the ecosystem in Yellowstone, (refer

Table 2.1 Complicated-Complex. Describes the Different Traits of Complicated and Complex Systems

Complicated	Complex
The whole is equal to the sum of the parts.	The whole is greater than the sum of the parts.
e.g. A mechanical/technical closed-loop system like a car or jet engine. Wheels in a car will turn to calculable angles based on the movement of the steering.	e.g. Open ecosystems like the forests of the Pacific Northwest. The role of salmon is critical, as it contributes a source of food for many Pacific species including bears, eagles and wolves; even after death they continue to contribute as they decompose into fertiliser for forests.
Impact of interventions can be controlled, and limited to parts of the system. System is predictable, and patterns are repeatable.	Interventions can lead to unintended consequences. Interaction in the system cannot be predicted, and cannot be completely replicated.
e.g. The process of fixing a flat tyre does not impact any other part of the machine.	e.g. When wolves were reintroduced to Yellowstone National Park in North America, they stabilised the ecosystem in ways that had not been foreseen. As an apex predator, they were able to control the population of deer, which ended up having a positive unintended consequence of stabilising river banks from less migration of hoofed creatures. However, the ecosystem of Yellowstone is unique in itself, and releasing wolves into other national parks will not necessarily create the same effect.
System has governing constraints.	System has enabling constraints.
e.g. The speed and engine power in a car is subject to the level of gears.	e.g. All ecosystems function based on some broad, enabling constraints such as how they organise around the apex predator who support species control, and ecosystem balance. However, it will go through periods where there will be more or less specific species. But a healthy ecosystem self-organises and self-regulates, and is not controlled.

to Table 2.1 above). We have to take a more experimental approach, try different probes in the system and be open to surprise.

> Something we may think to be insignificant (a casual remark, a joke, a tone of voice) may change everything. Conversely, the grand five-year plan, the result of huge effort, may retrospectively turn out to be meaningless. This is not an argument against proper planning; we have to plan. The point is just that we cannot predict the outcome of a certain cause with absolute clarity. [15]

ENHANCING ADAPTIVITY AND RESPONSE-ABILITY

Many of the trends of current transformation practices are in recognition of the fact that the competitive edge many businesses have traditionally gained from "scalable efficiency models" are no longer sustainable. John Hagel, the Founder and co-Chairman of Deloitte's Centre for the Edge, has described this fundamental Big Shift as organisations recognising the need to move from the "scalable efficiency models" founded on assumptions of complicated, stable systems to "scalable learning models" founded on complex adaptive systems, responding to greater levels of uncertainty. Whereas a complicated approach to change is for institutions to react to market pressures by getting more efficient at ever-larger scale, Hagel contends that the institutions with the greatest chance of succeeding in the future will be driven by scalable learning [16].

Scalable learning involves developing organisational architecture, policies and incentives that support everyone to think about creating new value for the business, not just the people at the strategic and executive core. By affording everyone in the organisation – from workers on the factory floor, to vendors and partners, to the front-line sales teams – to think about identifying problems and how to solve them, and how to respond to customer need in value-enhancing ways, the organisation is better set up to become responsive and adaptive. This is the push we have been seeing for more learning organisations [16, 17] from massive retailers like Walmart, to pharmaceutical giants like Novartis, that are now cultivating cultures underpinned by curiosity and on-going development.

This is taking place alongside moves to distribute leadership and decision-making across the organisation, and particularly to afford employees closest to the action and learning edge to respond and affect organisational change and strategy. We see this in management literature and examples from organisations as diverse as the military, in Gen. Stanley McChrystal and his colleagues' work on developing team-of-teams empowered with distributed autonomy that can better respond to Al Qaeda's decentralised network brand of warfare in Iraq [18], and appliance companies such as Haier, who preach a RenDanHeYi model that allows small teams at the edge of the organisation to create micro-businesses and evolve independently as they need to respond to emergent customer need [19].

In sum, roadmaps are attempts at simple stories that are built from a complicated, cause-and-effect world. As change is underway, and particularly in this environment where change is about allowing more latitude for organisations to learn and adapt, as well as distribute leadership and autonomy to the edge, a complex adaptive lens is more appropriate. We need to understand the emergent realities of what change sets off. The roadmap is a starting point, rather than a true-North artefact.

PLANNED APPROACHES TO CHANGE

In this section, we will be reviewing the different approaches to planning change. In so doing, we will also discuss the issues with each of the approaches, and provide recommendations for enhancing the evolvability of organisational transformation plans.

THE "BIG BANG" APPROACH

To introduce this approach, we quote John Hagel who put it succinctly,

> The top-down, big-bang approach is usually what you see when a senior leader gets inspiration and conviction that a transformation is necessary. They go in and say, 'We have to change everything. As we are a large organisation, it will take a lot of money and time, but trust me, at the end of all this, wonderful things will happen.' What this executive has done was put a bulls-eye on their back and invited the immune

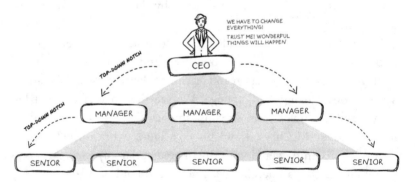

Figure 2.1 Big Bang Approach depicts a traditional top-down, big-bang approach where change is leader-initiated and led, with a typical waterfall cascade of change imagined.

system and antibodies to attack. They come out, crush it, and the academic studies show that most large-scale transformation efforts, anywhere from 70 to 85 percent, fail to achieve any of their objectives. [16]

This approach is fraught with heavy risk as it assumes that the transformation initiatives will pan out exactly as assumed, and that the entire organisation and individuals have the readiness to change in a uniform manner.

Hagel references an immune system and antibodies that come out to play when people and systems are threatened with change. This draws from the work of organisational psychologists from the Harvard Graduate School of Education. Robert Keegan and Lisa Lahey – immunity to change [20]. In their work, they describe why people in general are resistant to change, and how at an organisational level, this collective resistance makes large-scale change all the more difficult. Oftentimes, it is easy to pin the fault on a poor communication of purpose, or poorly implemented changes, however, the reality of change is that it is just that difficult. At a personal level, they describe the issue of competing commitments in people as change requires people to take risks, and shift their identity. Oftentimes, transformation also requires us to shift productivity into adaptive efforts, and this competes with how organisations have measured performance. The immunity is there to protect people and the systems they are used to. These antibodies can be conditioned and coached to adapt, however, too big and dramatic a change sets off the strongest antibodies.

There are purported success stories of organisational transformations that have followed such an approach. For example, in 2013, PayPal apparently moved their 510 cross-functional teams from Waterfall to Agile within less than a year. They moved from project-driven to product-line discipline in order to develop clear accountability and a more intense customer focus. Productivity and profitability rose significantly. Their journey has been widely shared across industry [21] as an example of a successful big-bang approach to transformation. We note, however, that PayPal is a digital native company focused on delivering software, and was transitioning into another digital native culture and model of Agile delivery. Older companies with more complex business models and operating structures, and entrenched cultures will likely not have had the same experience.

In most cases, the organisation has new department names, and adopts a new vocabulary that senior management preaches, but does not change their culture or actual ways of working. Success stories such as PayPal's are rare. Big Bang approaches may work better in smaller enterprises, or in circumstances where a major unforeseen crisis threatens the survival of the enterprise.

THE "INCUBATOR" APPROACH

This metaphor draws from the concept of incubating eggs in the form of alternate business ideas and comes from the innovation and venture capital world. While there are many definitions of incubation, most commonly, people think of incubation as corporations supporting internal start-ups with funding as well as social capital and existing infrastructure. That is, the internal startup also has access to a company's existing strengths, and can tap into its existing network of customers and partner ecosystems. This startup incubates ideas, approaches and business models that could help the company to move or expand into new or adjacent markets, industries and verticals.

Figure 2.2 Incubator Approach depicts the traditional egg metaphor of incubator models that fund and protect internal start-ups to cultivate new ideas safely away from the pressures of business-as-usual.

The incubation approach applied to change and transformation is where change is not directly introduced into the existing system, but a new system is set up to function in parallel to the existing one. This new system is operationally separate and designed to work based on the envisioned future state. For example, if PayPal had taken an incubator approach to its Agile transformation, they would have set up new teams that follow Agile ways of working, without disrupting the existing methods of delivery in the main organisation. They would then slowly integrate the new ways of working, or shift the centre of the organisation from the existing core to the incubated system. This approach is usually chosen when the constraints in the system are believed to be too severe.

The idea here is to create a new attractor in the system. It is also useful when the organisation has a very low appetite for change and disruption in its current environment.

The simple story of incubating change sounds like a way to slowly release new change agents and to cultivate new antibodies receptive to the change. However, organisations often experience issues with integrating the incubator and the existing system.

When the changes that have been incubated are introduced into business-as-usual (BAU), the issue is that that tends to trigger organisational antibodies. At a system level, there is often an "(mis)alignment

Figure 2.3 Incubator Approach – BAU watching from afar depicts a system of introducing new ways of working or innovation as separate from business-as-usual so the ideas under incubation are insulated from the pressures of regular business.

trap". The incubator is operating in the future state, whereas the rest of the enterprise is still in the current state. The existing system often also has a stronger culture based on its history and the memory of the system. This is a much stronger attractor than the incubator. This is the same issue that large organisations experience when trying to acquire start-ups to benefit from their innovative culture and ideas. Organisations assume that this new energy will infect the existing system. However, the gravitational pull of the existing culture is often much stronger than that of the new acquisition and subsumes it.

To improve the chances of an incubator model working, we recommend an approach of selective coupling when introducing new ideas. Integration is troublesome when eggs are incubated in an unintegrated satellite system. To improve the chances of integrating new ideas at a later stage, we recommend an approach that incubates eggs in a manner that protects them, but still keeps them close to business-as-usual, as well as to selectively couple innovation/change efforts with business-as-usual to allow for both to adjust and adapt to each other.

The incubator model draws from a culture of venture capital that is about making multiple parallel bets, rather than a steady investment in ensuring the success of a prescribed change journey. Research that has come out of the National Venture Capital Association in the United States estimates that about three-quarters of venture-backed startups fail. Venture capitalists however, "bury their dead very quickly", and

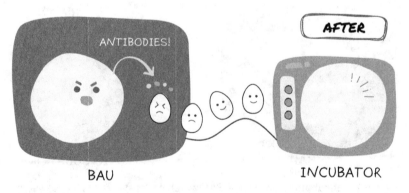

Figure 2.4 Organisational Antibodies Triggered depicts a system's natural resistance to orchestrated change being triggered when ideas are introduced into business as usual after a process of incubation.

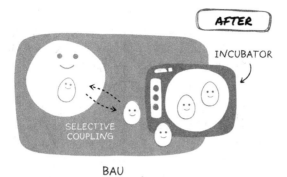

Figure 2.5 Selective Coupling depicts a process of careful coupling of incubated ideas with business-as-usual to allow for both business-as-usual as well as the change efforts to adjust and adapt to each other.

tend to emphasise the success and not talk about the failures at all [22]. The approach is deliberately set up for the incubation of multiple different ideas in parallel, with the hope that one out of four will bring the returns that will cover the failure in the other three. Incubators are useful when the journey is underway, and we have to run multiple experiments (knowing that many will fail) to see how the patterns unfold as we are moving along, and to utilise the learnings to adapt. They are great for exploration and prototyping to understand what might yield success, but not necessarily well suited as an approach for designing your whole journey.

THE "PHASED" APPROACH

The most common among the three traditional approaches is the approach to divide the transformation journey into phases, with each phase having a specific focus area of change. The four main phases of each transformation journey begin with a "Show" phase, designed to demonstrate the value of the stated change. Once the value has been demonstrated, the focus then "Shifts" to changing mindsets and culture of the organisation to better support the broader change. Once there is momentum that builds from this, the organisation can then refocus their efforts to "Scale" the change across the enterprise. The journey, however, will require the organisation to instil practices that "Sustain" the desired behavioural changes and culture. This is supported by ongoing streams of work which enable the overall

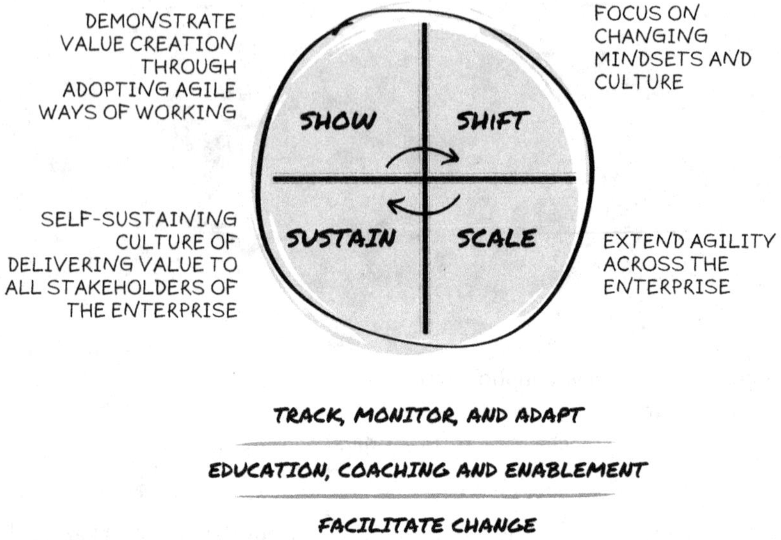

DEMONSTRATE
VALUE CREATION
THROUGH
ADOPTING AGILE
WAYS OF WORKING

SHOW   SHIFT

FOCUS ON
CHANGING
MINDSETS AND
CULTURE

SELF-SUSTAINING
CULTURE OF
DELIVERING VALUE TO
ALL STAKEHOLDERS OF
THE ENTERPRISE

SUSTAIN   SCALE

EXTEND AGILITY
ACROSS THE
ENTERPRISE

TRACK, MONITOR, AND ADAPT

EDUCATION, COACHING AND ENABLEMENT

FACILITATE CHANGE

Figure 2.6 Phased Approach depicts the Show-Shift-Scale-Sustain process of phasing transformation initiatives.

transformation: (1) tracking, monitoring and adapting, (2) education, coaching and enablement, and (3) change facilitation. These activities remain constant across all phases of the transformation [23].

Illustrates an example of a phased approach for an Agile transformation initiative.

In Complex systems, we cannot determine the end state, and therefore the focus is on how we begin. In this approach, it is recommended that the first phase to "Show" the change be done on a "thin slice" of the organisation. What this means is that the change should be done on a slice of the organisation that covers a full spectrum of a value stream or product, either partially or fully so we can impact the organisation across its operations.

The following is an example of a "thin slice" approach.

Our client was a non-banking finance company (NBFC), who is in the business of collecting deposits and lending.

The company has five lines of business:

1. Vehicle Loans
2. Home Loans
3. Personal Loans

4. Small Business Loans
5. Consumer Deposits

Their business had a four-stage process that was used to guide their launch of new products and services for their clients. These four stages include:

1. Ideation: This stage includes collecting ideas for new products and new features for existing products, validating and prioritising them, budgeting and capacity allocation.
2. Development: This stage includes converting the idea into solution-product development/enhancement, these include activities such as regulatory approvals, pre-launch marketing activities, training staff and external agencies who source business.
3. Sales: This stage includes launching the product in the market.
4. Servicing: This stage includes servicing the borrowers during the tenure of the loan/deposit and managing repayments of the loan/deposit.

The company's idea-to-realisation cycle time was on an average 13 months, which was resulting in them falling behind competition.

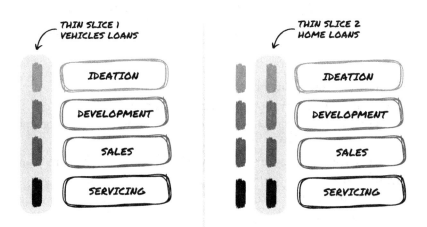

Figure 2.7 Thin Slices depicts the four-stage process adopted by this client, and how we chose thin slices across each stage and part of the process to begin transformation and change processes in small slices across the full spectrum of the delivery cycle.

They decided to take a thin-slice approach to implementing change, and selected vehicle loans line as the first thin slice.

The thin slice is meant to help us discover how the organisational antibodies will fire early in the transformation journey, so we can adjust the roadmap and approach. In this case, the client utilised a new product to create a container for the thin slice. This new product was a "top-up loan" facility that allows the customer to borrow more money from their existing loans based on loan quantums that had already been paid up for.

The thin-slice approach was a useful experimental space that helped the client to learn more about the "antibodies" and potential pitfalls that they had to watch out for before they extended their transformation process. Some of the learnings included the realisation that providing flexible loan facilities meant that they needed to make major changes to their annual budgeting cycle, which was the key reason for the long cycle time. Their budgeting cycles needed to be adjusted from annual to more frequent cadences to support greater adaptativity. They also realised that their IT systems and infrastructure needed modernisation to support this product. The company also faced backlash from their sourcing agents, who felt threatened that this product would impact their commission if the borrower chose to apply online.

These learnings guided the company to make the appropriate interventions before scaling the change across the rest of the organisation.

Following are some key considerations when deciding on the thin slice.

- Potential to create high business value/impact
- Medium complexity, both technical and functional
- Ease of taking the product/features to the customers, post-development

If the enterprise is very large, it may introduce change in more than one thin slice, which could include multiple product lines and geographies. Some key factors that should be considered while defining the scope and themes of the different phases are:

- Business priorities as they relate to desired dependencies on the transformation
- Current pain points

- Nature and rigidity of organisational constraints
- Appetite of the organisation for metabolising disruption, and impact on business as a whole
- Dependencies between actions across value streams

One of the glaring issues with this approach is that it is not always easy to "slice" an organisation in the manner that has been described. Because of the deeply entangled nature of complex adaptive systems, there is no neat slice. The relationships and networks cut across simple value streams, and are overlaid with informal networks and nodes of influence. Or, to borrow a metaphor from Alicia Juarrero, a philosopher on Complex Dynamics, complex adaptive systems present more like "bramble bushes in a thicket" [24].

The Show and Shift stages are also subject to heavy manipulation. Where there is a need to demonstrate the value of change, it is often easy to select and pilot with a group that is susceptible to the desired change, who might game the outcomes. Such issues have been well documented with the experiment conducted at the Hawthorne Works factory in the 1920s, where the organisation commissioned a study to determine if its workers would become more productive in higher or lower levels of light. The workers' productivity seemed to improve whatever changes were made, but slumped when the study ended. It turned out that the workers modified their behaviour and productivity in response to the awareness of being observed. This Hawthorne Effect is well documented and pilots designed to "Show the value of change" often experience the same types of effect [25].

That said, the phased approach does lend itself better to an organisation's ability to sense, adapt and respond in a transformation journey, if the attitude maintained is one of consistent learning and experimentation. We will discuss this in greater detail in the next Chapter where we talk about enhancing evolvability.

APPROACHES FOR EMERGENT CHANGE

Whilst transformation requires planning, it also requires planning for emergence, and maintaining a general attitude of adaptability and response-ability. We have reviewed some traditional approaches to planned change. In this section, we discuss recommended approaches to unplanned emergence. One of the key differences between the planned approach of complicated systems, and the emergence that we see in complex adaptive systems is that in complex systems we recognise we cannot define a future state.

A "VECTOR-BASED" THEORY OF CHANGE

In complicated systems the level of constraints are high and this makes behaviour predictable. You can therefore define the ideal future state, and then try to close the gap. In complexity, however, the constraints enable the system to provide some coherence, but allow for variation. It is therefore more helpful to describe the current state and understand what the evolutionary potentials are in the present. This is what Dave Snowden, Founder and Chief Scientific Officer of the Cynefin Co., describes as a "vector-based theory of change" [26]. Transformation is a journey of discovering "adjacent possibilities[1]", and understanding how we can nudge towards them.

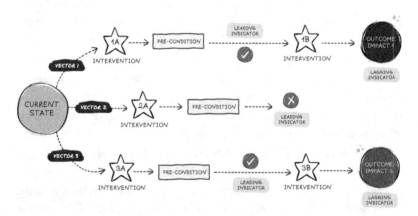

Figure 2.8 Vector Theory of Change depicts identifying possible vectors of change based on the possibilities presented by the current state, whilst maintaining mindfulness of the need to manage constraints and pre-conditions. We implement a portfolio of small interventions that might nudge toward the direction of change, and leading indicators need to be identified ahead of time to assess if these early interventions are working. Where the leading indicators provide evidence that the small experiments are working, they are augmented. Where the indicators provide no evidence of success, the experiments are stopped.

A vector is movement that has direction and speed/magnitude, rather than defined outcomes. Snowden suggests that vector-based targets are more useful for complex adaptive systems, particularly as complex systems have dispositions and display tendencies, and not linear casualties. It is, therefore, more helpful to ask questions like "Where are we now? Where is the system showing propensity for change, and what kind of change? Where are the energy gradients in the system most predisposed to shifts?" rather than "What outcomes do we want, and how do we reach them?".

Once the pathways in the system are identified, we then look for "stepping stones" that can be used. These are parallel interventions and experiments that help us to nudge toward the directions identified. Feedback loops need to be set up to determine how the landscape is shifting and developing. We augment efforts to support successful experiments, and only in ways the system indicates propensity for change to take effect. This is akin to Deng Xiaoping's famous metaphor for how China would navigate its reopening to the world. In the 1970s, Deng Xiaoping announced the intention for China to navigate from a closed, centrally planned economy to a more open and market-driven one. With the memory and history of the system, and the scale and variability of the country, they knew it would not be a straightforward task. His reform program subscribed to a philosophy of "crossing the river by feeling the stones".

This is a radically different approach to transformation planning, which in our experience, most organisations find hard to tolerate as it differs too greatly from the approaches we are used to. This also does not lend itself well to mid-term projections that are required for planning and budgeting. However, the wisdom of meeting the system where it is, and then finding ways to co-evolve with it is critical to bear in mind, and should be folded into the transformation journey to accompany the plan, as well as provide course corrections. Although it sounds similar to the Incubator model, this approach recognises that we are working directly within the system but in "safe-to-fail" experimental ways. It is not a separate "test environment". In complexity, we learn through action, and find ways to engage the system's response, rather than incubate from it. (We discuss this vector-theory of change in more detail in Chapter 4.)

DISCIPLINED NESTING

Insofar, we have referred to the organisation's transformation journey as though it is <u>one</u> distinct initiative. However, in all likelihood, organisations will experience the planned journey as a starting point that outlines the purpose and direction of change, and the emergent transformation as multiple disparate but coherent smaller initiatives that help the organisation amble in the stated trajectory. It is therefore important to cultivate discipline in how to nest initiatives within the larger transformation, as well as with each other. Needs resulting from the change will emerge as messy patterns, and there is the job of constant sensemaking to understand how they map into the journey, and how to act and nest them together so they have coherence. The outcome from such sensemaking might be a need to do some initiatives in sequence, but the sequential logic is not immediately apparent as we navigate the patterns.

This is one of the insights shared by Jeffrey Immelt, who was the Chairman of General Electric from 2001 to 2017, and who architected

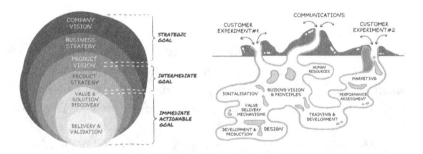

Figure 2.9 Planning Onion (left) depicts an example of a disciplined nesting approach that follows a Planning Onion, where different layers of goals and strategies are layered neatly. Whilst this is useful for presenting ideas in a neat and easy-to-communicate way, it does not accurately capture the process of managing through the emergence of transformation in a complex adaptive system. **Emergent Nesting (right)** depicts an example of disciplined nesting as an Ant Nest where needs across the system emerge as the journey is underway. The vision and strategies guide the design, but nesting needs to emerge through self-organisation of the system. The plan needs to adapt to accommodate these emergent needs, as do the flows of resources and leadership support[2].

GE's transformation into a technology-driven industrial company. GE is a 130-year-old company, with massive and complex operations across multiple business lines. When they first embarked on the journey, digital and industrial had just started to become a portmanteau term. At the end of Immelt's tenure at GE, he shared his reflections on the transformation that he had shepherded, and remarked on the importance of being "disciplined about nesting initiatives within one another—showing how each one fits with the rest—and staying away from new ideas that don't fit". Initiatives are always interconnected, and in leading transformations, there is a job of bringing them together that is on-going [28].

The change of the business impacts across the value chain, and into the way planning cycles and reviews are done. One of the core values that GE adopted during its transformation was to "Deliver results in an uncertain world". What this meant was that the cadence of the business became much faster. In response, the transformation team recognised that anything annual in review no longer made sense. Their planning cycles changed, and product iteration became continuous. This continuous iteration and reflection also continued into careers, strategy and business outcomes. Immelt shares that GE got rid of their legendary Session C process for succession planning – an annual ritual that had barely changed since its introduction in the 1970s. The career planning sessions became more frequent, and GE now calls them "people days" They changed the performance-development approach to one focused on giving people the feedback they want and need to produce better outcomes for customers.

We have found that in organisational transformations, one of the strongest constraints that change runs up against is an outdated performance assessment system. Whilst people recognise the assessments do not support the new values and learnings that have come with change, and appreciate the need for a rethink, there is also anxiety that without ratings and rankings there is no way to demonstrate progression and merit. The education system is one of the most outdated systems in the world, and suffers from exactly this same "competing commitment". We need to be coherent and nest transformation initiatives across the journey from customer value to your people; from strategy to portfolio. Otherwise, it bakes in its own immunity to change.

However, Immelt also cautions that this discipline of nesting, and saying no to initiatives that don't fit have to be managed against the openness to learning and pivoting. He describes a need to manage this paradox carefully. In his words,

> One of the hardest challenges in driving change is allowing new information to come in constantly and giving yourself the chance to adapt while still having the courage to act and push people forward. There's a tension: Even as you're making a major commitment of resources, you've got to be open to pivoting on the basis of what you learn, because you're unlikely to get the strategy perfect out of the gate. Nothing we've done has ever turned out exactly as it began.

FOCUS ON ENHANCING EVOLVABILITY AND NOT SUCCESS/FAILURE

With the sale of parts of GE Digital in 2021 and what was left of it absorbed by GE Power, there continues to be debate as to whether GE's Digital Transformation is a success or failure. However, these kinds of conversations beg the point of transformation. Transformation is any organisation's efforts to enhance its on-going evolvability. These debates try to wrap these efforts into a simple pass/fail story, and assume evolution is a journey to another terminal state. "Success or failure" cannot be determined by whether a business that sprung from those efforts does well, or gets sold for parts. Digital is one episode in any organisation's on-going journey to survive and thrive, and that is IF they manage to enhance their evolvability to meet the next challenge.

As a Wall Street Journal post-mortem explains, the development of GE Digital might have been premature as its own business line. "Instead of charging a small team with developing the best product and then letting the operation grow with the product's evolution, GE set up a huge organisation that wasn't quite needed yet". However, on a portfolio to strategy level of analysis, GE was able to benefit from the efforts to digitise and automate many of its business processes to generate savings [29]. Although GE Digital as a business failed, the learnings and adaptive practices it generated helped GE to achieve that next level of value where their processes were reimagined to support their vision of becoming a digital-industrial business.

MIND THE PLOT-TWIST

To evolve is to consistently mutate.

In Darwin's "On the Origin of Species" and "The Descent of Man", he makes clear references to vestigial organs in the human body that were left over as the species evolved. These evolutionary remnants represent a function that was critical for survival in the past, but became non-functional over time.

The appendix has often been cited as one such example. However, evolutionary biologists and surgical researchers are now challenging this assumption. Recent research reveals that the appendix has actually evolved 32 times among mammals. Its structure contains a particular type of tissue belonging to the lymphatic system which carries the white blood cells that help fight infections. It turns out that the monkey tail we had assumed was vestigial and an evolutionary remnant actually helps protect our beneficial gut bacteria when a serious infection strikes [30]. However, just as we cut off an appendix when it is infected to protect the rest of our system, we should not call it failure when we sell off a part of a company or close down a project that was a learning experiment. Sometimes that's precisely the kind of adaptation we need.

A complex adaptive system is larger than the sum of its parts. Having to sell off a business line, or close off an unsuccessful project do not simply represent the loss in terms of investment-to-date. This type of simple story betrays the learning and adaptive advantages that were gained through the process.

NOTES

1 With credit to evolutionary biologist Stuart Kauffman, from whom this term originated. Kauffman used it to explain how powerful biological innovations such as sight and flight came into being. More recently, Steven Johnson, showed that it's also applicable to science, culture, and technology. The core of the idea: People arrive at the best new ideas when they combine prior (adjacent) ideas in new ways.

2 "The intricacy and diversity of social insect structures are evocative of humans. However, they are constructed by completely different rules. Unlike man-made structures, which are usually made up of characteristic and standardised units assembled in exact sequence, more irregular parts make up social insect structures, and their assembly is the result of self-organising distributed processes, with little or no supervision. As a result, they are less standardised in structure, but more able to adjust conformation to changes…" [27]

REFERENCES

[1] Jennifer Garvey Berger. (8 Nov 2019) "Trapped by simple stories: When our instinct for a coherent story kills our ability to see a real one", in *Cultivating Leadership* blogpost. Accessed 16 Mar 2023. https://www.cultivatingleadership.com/uncategorized/2019/11/trapped-by-simple-stories-when-our-instinct-for-a-coherent-story-kills-our-ability-to-see-a-real-one

[2] Jennifer Garvey Berger. (2019) *Unlocking Leadership Mindtraps: How to thrive in Complexity*. Stanford University Press.

[3] Rune Todnem. (2005) "Organisational change management: A critical review", in *Journal of Change Management* (5: 4, 369–380).

[4] Margrit Liebhart & Lucia Garcia-Lorenzo. (2010) "Between planned and emergent change: Decision maker's perceptions of managing change in organisations", in *International Journal of Knowledge, Culture and Change Management* (10: 5, 214–225).

[5] Edwards Kasper, Prætorius Thim & Nielsen Anders Paarup. (2020) "A model of cascading change: Orchestrating planned and emergent change to ensure employee participation", in *Journal of Change Management* (20: 4, 342–368).

[6] Patrick Dawson. (1994) *Organisational Change: A Processual Approach*. Chapman Press.

[7] John P. Kotter. (2012) *Leading Change*. Harvard Business Review Press.

[8] John P. Kotter, Vanessa Akhtar & Gaurav Gupta. (2021) *Change: How Organisations Achieve HardtoImagine Results in Uncertain and Volatile Times*. Wiley.

[9] Haridomos Tsoukas & Robert Chia. (2002) "On organisational becoming: Rethinking organizational change", in *Organizational Science* (13: 5, 567–582).

[10] Wanda J. Orlikowski. (1996) "Improvising organizational transformation over time: A situated change perspective", in *Information Systems Research* (7: 1, 63–92).

[11] Ralph Stacey. (2005) (Ed.) *Experiencing Emergence in Organisations: Local Interaction and the Emergence of a Global Pattern*. Routledge.

[12] Ralph Stacey. (2001) *Complex Responsive Processes in Organisations: Learning and Knowledge Creation*. Routledge.

[13] Karl Weick. (2000) "Emergent change as universal in organisations", in M. Beer & N. Nohria (Eds.) *Breaking the Code of Change*. Harvard Business School Press.

[14] John Turner, Nigel Thurlow & Brian Rivera. (2020) *The Flow System: The evolution of Agile and Lean Thinking in an Age of Complexity*. University of North Texas Libraries.

[15] Paul Cilliers. (2000) "What can we learn from a theory of Complexity?", in *Emergence* (2: 1, 23–33).

[16] Peter High. (25 Jul 2016) "John Hagel: Scalable learning is the key differentiator fr enterprises of the future", in *Forbes Online*. Accessed 26 Mar 2023. https://www.forbes.com/sites/forbesdev/2023/02/28/increase-website-performance-with-three-metrics/?sh=49cfb0615fbd

[17] Peter Senge. (2006) *The Fifth Discipline: The Art & Practice of the Learning Organisation*. Doubleday.

[18] Gen. Stanley McChrystal, Tantum Collins, David Silverman & Chris Fussell. *Team of Teams: New Rules of Engagement in a Complex World*. Portfolio/Penguin.

[19] McKinsey Quarterly. (27 July 2021) "Starring the status quo: A conversation with Haier's Zhang Ruimin". Accessed 26 March 2023. https://www.mckinsey.com/capabilities/people-and-organizational-performance/our-insights/shattering-the-status-quo-a-conversation-with-haiers-zhang-ruimin#/

[20] Robert Keegan & Lisa Lahey. (2009) *Immunity to Change: How to Overcome it and Unlock the Potential in Yourself and Your Organisation.* Harvard Business Review Press.

[21] PayPal Enterprise Transformation Whitepaper. (2015) Accessed 27 March 2023. https://www.paypalobjects.com/webstatic/en_US/mktg/pages/stories/pdf/paypal_transformation_whitepaper_sept_18_2015.pdf

[22] Deborah Gage. (20 Sep 2012) "The venture capital secret: 3 out of 4 Start-Ups Fail", in *Washington Street Journal.* Accessed 27 March 2023.

[23] Sunil Mundra. (2018) *Enterprise Agility: Being Agile in a Changing World.* Packt.

[24] Alicia Juarrero. (2002) *Dynamics in Action: Intentional Behaviour as a Complex System.* Bradford Books.

[25] Rob McCarney, James Warner, Steve Iliffe, Robert van Haselen, Mark Griffin & Peter Fisher. (2007) "The Hawthorne effect: A randomised, controlled trial", in *BMC Medical Research Methodology* (7: 30).

[26] Linda Doyle. (Dec 2021) *Change & Complexity: Vector Theory of Change Whitepaper.* The Cynefin Co. (Accessed 28 March 2023).

[27] Guanghong Yang, Wei Zhou, Wenjun Qu, Wu Yao, Peng Zhu & Jing Xiu. (2022) "A review of ant nests and their implications for architecture", in *Architectural Design, Urban Science and Real Estate* (12: 22, 2225).

[28] Jeffrey Immelt. (Sep-Oct 2017) "How I Remade GE", in *Harvard Business Review Magazine.* Accessed (28 March 2023).

[29] Ted Mann & Thomas Gryta. (18 July 2020) "The dimming of GE's bold digital dreams", in *The Wall Street Journal.* Accessed (29 March 2023)

[30] Colin Barras. (12 Feb 2013). "Appendix evolved more than 30 times", in *Science.org: Evolution.* Accessed 29 March 2023. https://www.science.org/content/article/appendix-evolved-more-30-times

Three

INTRODUCTION

In March 2020, the whole world came to a remarkable standstill as we were all held hostage in our homes by a virus. It turned out, as GE Appliances (GEA) discovered, that when people stay at home, they tend to utilise their domestic appliances more than usual. They were cooking at home, and doing laundry more frequently. GEA realised that they needed to step up production. However, safety concerns meant that manufacturing had to be shut down.

> The company had to run the plants, but nobody had a clue how exactly to do it in the middle of a global pandemic... Plant managers had been invited to propose their own solutions and practical plans, coming up with six different options after a few weeks. Instead of letting the boss decide the proposal that looked most promising, the teams tested all of them to autonomously adhere to a final one that mixed features from multiple approaches. Meanwhile, at Ford Motors, the creation of a 100-page toolkit explaining how to run a plant required three months before any implementation was possible. A more bureaucratic culture and process required months to arrive at an initial solution, while GE Appliances was already busy experimenting with and learning from multiple possibilities. [1]

At this point, GEA was approximately 5 years into their transformation journey, to adopt and adapt the RenDanHeYi principles and operating system of their new parent company, Haier. Wait. What is that?

RenDanHeYi is a radical new incarnation of the modern organisation. Explained by Haier CEO,

> Zhang Ruimin, Ren (人) is a Chinese word that means people or person. We mainly use it to refer to employees within an organization. Dan (单) means orders, and here it represents the needs or demand of

DOI: 10.4324/9781003505433-4

users. Heyi (合一) means integration. So, we're talking about the fact that everyone, every employee, gets to create value for users. [2]

This principle of trying to integrate the organisation's strategy and operations with evolving customer needs was inspired by the aspiration of maintaining "zero-distance with the customer". To achieve this, Haier removed an intermediate layer of 12,000 employees who used to be organised across a bureaucracy which was seen as not adding customer value, and perversely buffering it instead. This was replaced by a decentralised, distributed network instead. The goal was a kind of "institutionalised autonomy": Autonomous teams that self-manage and coordinate themselves around user outcomes through dynamic contracts, in a largely flat structure. Teams have the authority to hire and fire, and work with who they like. Salaries are tied to micro-enterprise profitability, and therefore paid by customers. The strategy is created both from the top and the bottom. Sounds weird and chaotic?

That was exactly what Kevin Nolan, the CEO of GE Appliances thought when Haier had acquired GEA in 2016. His initial thought was "this is pure chaos". When Nolan spent time in China trying to learn from the source, Haier had no organisational charts to study. There was also no visible boss in charge. Their goals were not written, and their processes were unclear. Most of the basic organisational hygiene that he assumed were taken-for-granted truths for a functioning organisation of that size were missing. Even more astonishing was that the business results demonstrated tremendous growth. None of it fit Nolan's sensemaking frames. It was only when he allowed these frames to relax, did he realise how much of how we perceive of the organisation is built around centralisation, bureaucracy and control. He had to believe another type of organisation, developed around decentralised networks and autonomy was possible.

"It's actually not that hard. You just have to dare to let go—to give up control", he reflects [3].

ENABLING CONSTRAINTS AND EVOLVABILITY

RenDanHeYi is one example of a growing trend of complex adaptive modern organising principles that are emerging in response to the recognition of a need for organisations to remain evolvable. The company, Corporate Rebels, who describe themselves as "creators of a movement of individuals and organisations that inspire changes towards more engaging workplaces" have been travelling the world and studying organisations that have been implementing alternative models of organising and practising different ways of working, all of which aimed at developing better workplaces that can unleash the potential of their employees [4]. Through their study of 150+ companies pioneering these new practices, they have found 8 key trends.

These trends are a shift from (1) profit to Purpose and values, (2) pyramid and bureaucracies to Networks of teams, (3) directive leadership to Supporting leadership, (4) planning and prediction to Experiments and Adaptation, (5) rules and control to Freedom and Trust, (6) centralised authority to Decentralised decision-making, (7) secret and turf guarding to Transparency and collaboration and (8) activities and jobs built around job titles and descriptions, to cultivating Talent and mastery based on proclivities [5]. These trends all describe moving from the rigid and governing constraints of ordered and complicated systems, to the more enabling constraints of complex systems to encourage greater adaptivity and evolvability.

Enabling constraints as a term seems almost oxymoronic as we often think of constraints as things that hold things back, rather than enable. However, there is a very common-sense aspect to it that we intuit – for example, "good fences make good neighbours" as an idiom is easily understood. To better clarify the difference between constraints that govern and constraints that enable, Dave Snowden describes the difference between the exoskeletons and endoskeletons. An exoskeleton is like the external skeleton of an insect. These are often rigid shells that do not display much variation; however, inside the shell, things may change and vary. An endoskeleton is like a human spine that gives coherence to the human body, but does not contain it [6]. Whereas all insects of a particular species look fairly similar, you get huge amounts of variation in human bodies. We are able to develop varying degrees of muscle, and flexibility in sinew. This is of huge importance for how we architect and manage systems. For complex adaptive systems, we have to create enabling constraints that allow locally valid solutions to emerge within the framework. Snowden argues that people have tended to assume that all constraints must be governing constraints. This stifles a system's adaptive and transformative capacity, and overall evolvability.

In our day-to-day business, enabling constraints can take the form of time-boxes and cadences on work deliverables and review cycles as

CICADA SHELL

EXAMPLE OF AN EXOSKELETON THAT
ENCASES THE INSECT'S ORGANIC SYSTEM
AND IMPOSES AN EXTERNAL CONSTRAINT.

FISH BONES

EXAMPLE OF AN ENDOSKELETON THAT PROVIDES
AN ENABLING STRUCTURAL CONSTRAINT FOR THE
ORGANIC SYSTEM TO GROW AROUND, BUT DOES
NOT IMPOSE EXTERNAL CONSTRAINTS.

Figure 3.1 Containing Constraint (left) A cicada shell – example of an exoskeleton that encases the insect's organic system and imposes an external constraint. **Enabling Constraint (right)** Fish bones – an example of an endoskeleton that provides an enabling structural constraint for the organic system to grow around, but does not impose external constraints.

they provide a loose constraint for planning purposes. Writing a system's requirements, or the testing requirements it has to pass (i.e. test-driven development in software or product development work) are also examples of enabling constraints. However, the nuance of human-enforced constraints is that whilst these time-boxes and cadences begin as enabling constraints, organisations can often fall into the trap of enforcing them as hard endoskeletons that constrain work and behaviour in unhealthy ways. Similarly, even when new products or services are deemed ready by requirements-based testing, they often have to pass the true test of how the users and agents in the system interact with it. In product work, these are easier to observe. However, when we are dealing with systems-level transformation (i.e. strengthening a health or social system, policy work, energy transition) these will require us to keep our requirements emergent. The attitude toward regular and iterative stakeholder engagement, needs-gathering and consultative dialogue provide the enabling constraints.

FORCES OF EVOLUTION

Flip open any high school or pre-university level textbook on General Biology, and head to the sections that discuss Evolution. Four key forces are often described that drive evolution. These are mutation (a change in our DNA sequence), gene flow (the transfer of genital material from one pool to another), genetic drift (a process of variation)

and natural selection (survival and reproductive rate based on adaptability of species to environment). These, along with Snowden's metaphor of the spine as an enabling constraint, provide useful metaphors for thinking about the approaches that we need to adopt to support greater evolvability.

Evolvability is underpinned by the ability of the system to develop adaptive mutations to respond to change, as well as the ability for these mutations to be "heritable" and sustained. This response-ability denotes a kind of system health. If we look at the trends in transformation, we see terms like:

- Agility/agile: Colloquially used to describe the ability to move quickly and easily, and to change direction and accelerate/decelerate. Technically, it has been described by Jim Highsmith, co-author of the Agile Manifesto, as "the ability to both create and respond to change in order to profit in a turbulent business environment... and balance flexibility and stability" [7].
- Nimble: Colloquially used to describe the ability to be quick and light in movement and action. Technically, Kate Isaacs from MIT Sloan Executive Education, highlights its focus on teams that are flexible and fluid, with leadership distributed across many levels of authority. It also has a strong culture and leadership focus on "how to get culture off the wall and into the water" [8].
- Adaptive: Colloquially used to describe the ability to change to suit shifting conditions. Technically, it was described by Futurologist and author of The Adaptive Corporation (1985), Alvin Toffler, as incorporating 3 key attributes: (1) employees, departments, and groups collaborating effectively; (2) employees at all levels to network with others outside the organisation, gaining new sources of information and perspectives in the process; and (3) employees at all levels innovating and experimenting without fear of reprisal or marginalisation [9].

Toffler introduced these ideas in his infamous Toffler Report back in 1985. The ideas and need for organisations to maintain evolvability are not new. However, the ways forward, and "how" had not been popularly discussed in management approaches till the rapid acceleration in the past decade. In terms of the "how" to achieve this, we see terms like distributed decision-making, autonomous teams, distributed leadership and team-of-teams. This distribution of adaptive freedom to the edges of the organisation, as well as enhancing agency appear to be the metabolic mechanisms needed to maintain the health for evolvability. People need to be empowered and responsible to lead. They need to be able to make decisions, take action and communicate without unwieldy bureaucratic chain-of-command gates. Leaders also need to be able to solicit new ideas at all levels, know when and how to create business proposals, and how to translate new ideas into plans and action.

EVERYONE, EVERYWHERE, ALL AT ONCE – LEADING FOR EVOLVABILITY

Prof. Deborah Ancona, the Founder of the MIT Leadership Centre has identified three key leadership archetypes that are necessary to support the cultivation of an organisational culture that encourages the freedom to grow as a leader at every level of an organisation: "Entrepreneurial leaders, typically concentrated at lower levels of an organisation, create value for customers with new products and services; collectively, they move the organisation into unexplored territory. Enabling leaders, in the middle of the organisation, make sure the entrepreneurs have the resources and information they need. And architecting leaders, near the top, keep an eye on the whole game board, monitoring culture, high-level strategy, and structure. [10]

In Ancona's research, she has focused on what she terms "X-teams": Externally oriented groups that reach out beyond their boundaries to learn, develop alliances within the organisation, and connect outwards beyond the organisation, into the larger ecosystem [11]. Placing the research focus here highlights the importance of considering the porosity of the system. CAS are not closed systems – but they are also not without boundaries. The key is recognising that boundaries are porous, and you require boundary spanners across all levels. The three leadership archetypes – entrepreneurial, enabling and architecting – help to support boundary spanning, and recognise the porosity of the system.

The real change tends to happen at the edges with the Entrepreneurial leaders who are closest to the frontline. They have the shortest feedback loops with customers and evolving situations on the ground, and are best equipped to decide a response. The middle of the organisation is meant to provide support and enabling leadership that facilitates resources and information to support these strategic front-line needs, and the top is meant to architect something that can support the whole. This is an organisational model that is upside down and inside-out from what we have grown accustomed to. Traditional organisation is based on people performing tasks that they learned to perform rote. However, as things radiate out from central leadership, people begin to lose the bigger picture "why". Today organisations are too complex for management to do all the thinking, and we require distributed leadership to better support adaptability, and sensemaking across the system to understand how patterns are shifting in our operating environment.

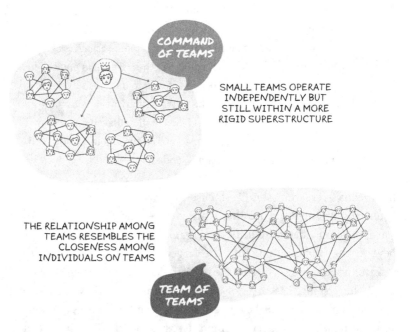

Figure 3.2 Command of Teams (top) depicts working through teams that remain centrally coordinated and with limited connections across teams. In this approach, leadership is still communicating decisions and pushing them down. **Team-of-Teams (below)** depicts a network of teams with interpersonal relationships of trust and information sharing encouraged across teams, and team members from other teams. Rotations across teams and units are needed to forge relationships across the organisation to augment networks of informal leadership and influence, and their corresponding followership.

In Gen. Stanley McChrystal's reflections on his leadership of the Joint Special Operations Command in Iraq, he described how he often had to green light operations and decisions for troops whom he knew understood the problem on the ground much better than he did. He described that this created an unnecessary impediment that took up time and reduced the optimal adaptive capabilities of the force, making them clumsier than their enemy. As Architect, what he set out to create was a "shared consciousness". He did this through sharing information in an open way that encouraged everyone in the organisation to understand the whole, and understand the thought process behind decisions.

He made this clear that this was not simply about communicating decisions and pushing them down, but sharing how decisions are considered, and what influenced them. In his book, *Team-of-Teams* [12], he describes how the military solved for this by holding weekly live meetings with the entire task force where everyone could see the leaders' thought process, and contribute where relevant. New types of meetings that went beyond a "need-to-know" basis meant that information flow in organisations was changing. The old adage that "information is power" means that distributing information more widely allows leaders across levels to become more empowered, and for shorter feedback loops. He then sought to carefully weave a network of networks. Rotations were set up across teams and units to forge relationships across the organisation to augment networks of informal leadership and influence, and their corresponding followership. He was mindful that competitive performance assessment and resource allocation systems mean that teams will try to optimise themselves, with little concern of the detriment to other teams. As a result, the whole system is not working together. His architecting had to go beyond just information sharing, and also into the relationships necessary for the building of empathy and trust.

He also realised that distributed leadership cannot work without empowering people to execute. If we sing the gospel of distributing leadership and decision-making, but people keep running up against hard constraints such as rigid approval processes, or punitive cultural reactions to independent actions, then people quickly learn to give performances, rather than to properly perform. We have to empower people with space to make decisions and take action without needing explicit approval. For example, flexible budgeting which provides allowance for experimentation, or providing loose guidelines for experimentation allow people to execute on ideas, and better create a culture of distributed leadership. It is important to note, however, that we should not empower people to make decisions before we implement shared consciousness as it is critical to have people understand the strategic intent. Decisions can then be made within a clear understanding of each person's role and accountability as it can relate to strategic intent.

Micro-enterprises at Haier

This approach focuses on supporting the entrepreneurial aspirations of each employee. Micro-enterprises are essentially groups of employees who self-select and self-organise. This can be done through spontaneous grouping or groups attracting the right talent through marketing their ideas in the organisational ecosystem. These micro-enterprises

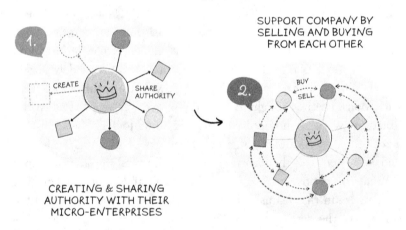

Figure 3.3 Micro-Enterprises depicts the entrepreneurial set-up of Haier that has removed intermediating middle layers of bureaucracy, and has instead created an eco-system of micro-enterprises that form at the customer-facing end. Each micro-enterprise runs its own P&L, and is free to buy and sell services from across the ecosystem to create customer solutions. To support this, Haier has set up a digital platform that sits in the centre of the organisation, and helps support contracting between micro-enterprises. This is a form of the newly emerging model of "digitally enhanced directed autonomy" revolutionising how management is done in Chinese companies.

form at the customer-facing end, and employees take P&L responsibility. Their guiding principle is to create value for themselves, and cultivate lifelong Haier customers.

As these groups are responsible for their own P&L and decisions, the profits from their venture are shared across the team. These enterprises are connected through a technology platform to the people managing resources at the back end. People at both the front and back ends build communities of interest that work together to make sure customer needs are met quickly and effectively. These entrepreneurial teams are free to enlist the help of suppliers, other microenterprises, and other partners from within or outside the Haier group as they deem fit. These relationships also take the form of micro-contracts that determine the rights and responsibilities of different microenterprises, team members and stakeholders [2, 13].

This is a heavy entrepreneurial set-up, and because Haier chose to remove the middle layer of its bureaucracy, the middle has been replaced by what authors at the Harvard Business Review are now terming "digitally enhanced directed autonomy", or DEDA. These are digital platforms which sit in the centre of the organisation, and which help support the micro-enterprise contracting. The system sets clear bounded business objectives, but grants them the autonomy to pursue them as they believe is best. "Autonomy is not complete, nor is it given to everyone. It is directed exactly where it is needed, and what employees do with their autonomy is carefully tracked. The approach contrasts with the Western model of empowerment, which gives employees broad autonomy through reduced supervision" [14].

We discuss these two examples of team-of-teams and micro-enterprises as they provide sufficient contrast in organisation type and operating context, and who have operationalised the mechanisms of evolvability in their own way. The architects of both systems have to define and develop clear strategic intent (whether it is through "shared consciousness", or digitally bounded business objectives), and design systems that help to support them. In Team-of-Teams, the military cannot remove rank and file bureaucracy as radically as Haier did. However, it created enabling constraints and leadership through changing information flow, and providing what McChrystal terms "empowered execution". However, where the military's discipline, structure and McChrystal's new "shared consciousness" provided the

Joint Special Operations Command with Snowden's concept of the "spine", Haier utilises a digital platform solution to support contracting and resourcing.

ENHANCING YOUR ORGANISATIONAL EVOLVABILITY

Allow for Mutation

In both examples we have just discussed, as well as in the two organisations that Ancona studied (Xerox Palo Alto Research Centre and W.L. Gore.), the same patterns of allowing for self-organisation around emergence at the frontline were critical. Organisations need to mobilise people – employees, suppliers, cross-industry partners and independent developers and players – as well as cultivate a system that allows for continuous adaptability.

Complex Adaptive Systems respond to change through mutation. Sometimes these are deleterious, and sometimes they are adaptive. We cannot tell ahead of time the nature of the mutation. However, not allowing for mutation means an unresponsive and ill-adapting system. We have to relax constraints, and provide people with genuine autonomy within their operating contexts to make decisions and execute. Some organisations have provided skin-in-the-game to employees to cultivate a deeper level of stakeholdership.

A clear strategic intent needs to be in place and communicated, and enabling constraints put in place to allow the system to self-correct against the intent. Most organisations who are transitioning from a traditional model of control and bureaucracy often fear the "chaos" that will be unleashed from relaxing the system. However, when done correctly, and when people are empowered to act to impact on strategic intent, they begin to better appreciate their role and influence in the system. A networked approach to leadership requires followers to take more responsibility.

Stimulate Gene Flow

A networked and ecosystem approach works well when ideas, agents and resources are free to flow across the system. Having an abundance of ideas or resources is not productive if these are bottlenecked and unable to flow to find suitable energy outlets. In McChrystal's case, he stimulated a flow and exchange through rotations through different units. In Haier's case, team members self-select their team members. And the digital contracting system is set up in a manner where members continue to be compensated for their efforts even if they leave, so the compensation system is set up to encourage people to go where they can best utilise their potential and interests.

At Gore, the organisation boasts a "lattice" structure that is about maximising interconnection among associates. It highlights the more informal networks of relationships, information flow and influence. These lattices are designed to ensure (1) direct lines of communication from person-to-person across the organisation is possible, without the need of an intermediary, (2) no fixed assigned authority so roles can evolve according to need, (3) projects and ideas have sponsors, rather than "bosses", (4) natural leadership is enhanced based on willingness of others to follow, (5) objectives are set by those who have to make things happen and (6) tasks and functions are organised through commitment. The importance is that interaction is not hampered by bureaucracy, and teams are assembled based on knowledge and skills. Bill Gore describes the lattice as harnessing the power of the informal networks. "Every successful organisation has an underground lattice…where the news spreads like lightning, where people can go around the organisation to get things done" [15].

Bet on Natural Selection

Gene flow is further augmented by a type of "natural selection" process. Across manufacturers such as Haier, Xerox PARC and Gore, who work in different spaces, new products and services are dreamed up not by high-level strategists or "innovators" housed in a separate incubator, but by teams of employees. And, people are free to walk away if a project loses steam, or if they find a project they deem more valuable.

Beyond the self-emergence of these project/business ideas, the way teams form also demonstrates a principle of natural selection. Funding goes to the projects that are able to attract staffing; as success escalates, more resources flow in. At any given moment, the organisations always have multiple small bets being experimented on in parallel, and employees are choosing which ones to back. The company ecosystem becomes in and of itself a collective prediction market, as they have discovered that talent and interest tend to pool around good ideas and drain from bad ones [10].

Attune to Genetic Drift

Genetic drift refers to "the change in frequency of an existing variant in the population due to chance. Genetic drift may cause gene variants to disappear completely and thereby reduce genetic variation. It could also cause initially rare alleles to become much more frequent, and even fixed" [16]. This highlights the importance of being open to new patterns of emergence – that is, not all ideas or projects that were successful in the past will remain so, and the next mutation might take us by surprise.

As patterns in complex adaptive systems are always emergent, having a diversity of sensemaking is also critical to ensure we do not become pattern-entrained by previous success. We need to maintain mechanisms that allow for weak signal detection so we can exploit early patterns, as well as plan ahead for any early signals of "drifting".

Operationalising Organisational Evolvability

In this chapter, we have described the principles and mechanisms that help to enhance evolvability. In this section, we will be describing a general approach and attitude of continuous **Sense-Adapt-respond** that can help to support the operationalisation of an evolvable organisation.

The distributed leadership and networks that support evolvability require us to also develop a culture and operational system that allow for:

- **Sensemaking** – Incorporating diversity of perspectives across the system, especially those closest to the frontline of the organisation. Openness in allowing for creation and evolution of new meaning and understanding that will impact on how we frame the business support adaptation and response-ability. This might be small, incremental product level changes, or larger business-level responses to a shifting environment (i.e. moving from providing a product to experience, building a platform to an ecosystem). We cover sensemaking in greater detail in the next chapter, as it is one of the biggest debts that are created in transformation journeys.
- **Adaptation** – Affording the system and its agents the nimbleness and flexibility to make changes, and self-organise to realign priorities. We need to minimise friction in the operating model that might impede the speed of adaption (i.e. maintaining the right level

of granularity in how we define strategic priorities, cultivating a more responsive resourcing model).

- **response** – Transformation that enhances evolvability must be done from a systemic perspective and not optimised in parts. For example, if we have sensed a new need emerging and have designed some experiments to test ideas against the potential opportunity, but have to wait to get funding or approval through the annual budgeting process, the opportunity will be lost. The system needs to be able to respond when the adaptive move has been identified.

In Figure 3.4 below, we illustrate the Sense-Adapt-respond loop. You will note, however, that the Sense-Adapt loop is a more tightly coupled loop. This is because organisations are continuously learning and adapting. Traditional approaches to transformation and change management, however, have focused more on an organisation's formal "response" to managing in complexity and uncertainty. "In turbulent times where change is perpetual and relentless… organisations learn

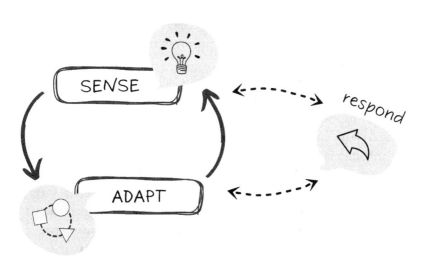

Figure 3.4 Sense-Adapt-Respond depicts the tight Sense-Adapt loop. Sense-Adapt is presented as a more tightly coupled loop as organisations are continuously learning and adapting. The loop has a small "r" that lag the ongoing Sense-Adapt cycle as it recognises that formal "responses" lag after a process of sensemaking and adaptation.

to respond more by sensing, improvising and adapting as they go; they rely more on practice-acquired sensitivities and dispositions to help them cope, adjust and adapt effectively." The evolveable organisation therefore recognises that the Sense-Adapt-repond loop has a small 'r' that lags the ongoing Sense-Adapt cycle, which is a natural survival instinct. And, in many cases, we have multiple small "responses" as we recognise the need for experimentation, as well as differentiated approaches across different parts of the business. We provide a case study around Coca-Cola to illustrate what we mean.

Case Study: New Coke

The introduction of New Coke in 1985 is one of the most infamous marketing blunders in the history of the beverage industry.

History

Coca-Cola had been the leading soft drink company for decades. However, by the early 1980s, its main competitor, Pepsi, had been gaining ground with the "Pepsi Challenge" marketing campaign, which claimed that consumers preferred the taste of Pepsi over Coke in blind taste tests.

Coca-Cola decided to address this challenge by reformulating its classic Coca-Cola recipe, which had been virtually unchanged since its creation in 1886. The company conducted extensive taste tests and concluded that consumers preferred a sweeter, smoother taste, which was more similar to Pepsi.

On 23 April 1985, Coca-Cola launched New Coke, a reformulated version with a different taste. Coca-Cola made a very bold move to discontinue the original Coke. However, they completely misjudged the strong emotional attachment consumers had to the original coke. Many consumers saw it as a tampering of a beloved American icon. This caused a massive backlash and public outcry, which forced Coca-Cola to bring back the original Coke within 79 days of the introduction of New Coke.

Analysis

If we were to utilise the Sense-Adapt-respond loops to analyse this case study, we see several issues with how Coca-Cola had mishandled their transformation strategy.

In the research and pre-introduction phase, they had attempted to do some "sensing" with their market research. However, their research had been based on a hypothesis that the brand value of Coke was linked fundamentally to taste as a factor. Their research hypotheses were shaped in response to their competitor's successful marketing strategy, rather than a genuine sensing of the factors that shaped their customer's preferences. The introduction of New Coke was based only on taste tests, in response to the Pepsi challenge. Their sensing was overly focused in one specific area, and on a flawed hypothesis. They also did not "adapt" by making small adjustments, but instead over-corrected with a large Response of altering their base recipe, and discontinuing the original Coke in parallel with the introduction of New Coke. This was a "big-bang" transformation response that was developed based on flawed sensing, and no organic adaptation.

The reaction to the withdrawal of traditional Coke was loud and clear. Angry customers launched protests and filed petitions demanding the return of the original Coke. The backlash received extensive media coverage which fuelled the controversy. These events had a negative impact on the stock price of Coca-Cola. The signals were so strong that Coca-Cola announced they were bringing back the original Coke just 79 days after its withdrawal.

This event, however, taught Coca-Cola a very valuable lesson about the perception of its brand. Following this, they have utilised the "Can't beat the real thing" slogan to great success, marketing itself as the original cola of the world. It has now branched off to create multiple flavours and varieties of cola (Cherry Coke, Vanilla Coke, Coke Zero), however, these are small and additive "responses" which experiment with multiple small hypotheses, and provide options for the consumer, rather than a big Response that seeks to completely alter the base recipe or image of the brand.

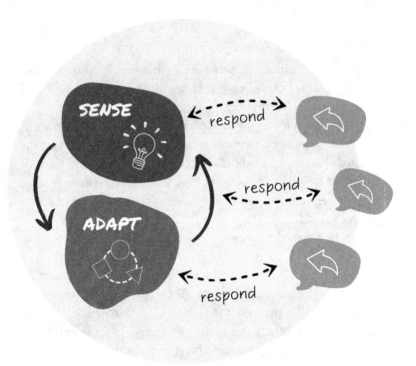

Figure 3.5 Sense-Adapt-Multiple Experiments depicts the small and additive "responses" which experiment with multiple small hypotheses, and provide options for the consumer, rather than a big Response.

BREAKING THE LOOP DOWN TO ITS PARTS

Sense

The effectiveness of our adaptive responses depends on the diversity, timeliness and openness of our sensing capability. Some key areas to cultivate Sensing are with our Customers, Competitors, the Technology landscape, Government policies and regulations. However, the weaker signals tend to coalesce in areas we had not expected. Therefore, a diversity of sense-makers serve the Sense capability best.

"Sense" is enhanced by:

- **Diversity of perspectives:** Sometimes the best ideas come from least-expected areas. Some organisations host regular competitions and student-internship programs that allow them to tap into the sensemaking of people outside the usual suspects. Find ways to bring in people who might give you the unarticulated perspectives (like inviting security guards to design shoes for comfort and usage over long periods). This also means we are consistently inviting and testing multiple hypotheses, with different perspectives on the issue.

- **The right feedback loops:** In the famous leaked email from Elon Musk to his Tesla employees, he stated that "communication should travel via the shortest path necessary to get the job done, not through the chain of command". The structure of your communications should be permeable to allow critical information to reach the relevant stakeholders quickly. Gore, the global material science company famous for its innovative culture has a lattice structure that is designed to ensure everyone in the organisation can reach anyone else should they wish to.

  The feedback loops we put in place should allow corroboration of patterns and signals across different parts of the organisation. Individual signals may appear insignificant but when combined with other signals can lead to emergence of a view that individual signals would not provide. Sensing needs to go from small signals to a bigger picture. This is the nesting and sensemaking work that Immelt, former CEO of GE, shared is critical for transformation journeys (see Chapter 2).

- **Psychological safety:** Amy Edmondson's research focused on clinical teams and the number of mistakes different teams made. Her work revealed that teams with a higher number of good outcomes actually made more mistakes than teams with fewer good outcomes. It was a surprising result, but after further investigation, Dr Edmondson discovered that in fact those teams with better outcomes were admitting more mistakes, whilst the teams with fewer good outcomes were more likely to hide theirs. Those teams felt safer to speak up about any concerns, mistakes or suggest ideas. The teams felt safe enough for members to take interpersonal risks [17]. Psychological safety contributes to higher-quality decision-making, group dynamics and interpersonal relationships. These support greater innovation, and more effective execution in organisations [18].

Adapt

Some key areas that need to be transformed to enhance adaptation are how we outline strategic priorities and align to purpose. We also need to be mindful about how we are designing our organisational processes (deliberately or unconsciously), as change and transformation often accumulate organisational debt. Aspects of existing structure, processes and policies become obsolete as we change and respond to the environment. Fumito Ueda, an award-winning designer, describes that we have a tendency when seeking to improve and enhance things, to design by addition. However, this means any changes we implement are simply additive to a system, and creates debt we have to maintain. He introduced a new design approach "Design by Subtraction", which encourages people to remove superfluous and extraneous parts in order to strengthen the core elements [19]. We have to be mindful of the "competing commitments" that bring about a system's immunity to change (see Chapter 2), and that we are consistently refining, and not simply adding to our system. We cover this in greater detail in Chapter 4.

"Adapt" is enhanced by:

- **Adaptable purpose, vision and values:** Purpose is seen as a company's reason for being, and the animating force for achieving organisational goals and desired outcomes, and provides a vision that people can rally behind during transformation. According to Kotter (see Chapter 2) to create purpose, it is important to "create urgency" around a change, and to develop and communicate a vision linked to that.

  Purpose often seems clear at the beginning, but begins to fragment when it is communicated, and re-interpreted by different people – particularly as the journey is underway. It therefore has to be broad enough to incorporate ongoing changes and interpretations over time and tensions, but also aligned enough to outcomes and objectives so people can link transformation outcomes and targets back to the rallying call. Distributing sensemaking and decision-making means that people will practise "adaptive justice" as they go along. We have to ensure the Purpose, Vision and Values are adaptable across the organisation's transformation journey.

Granularity refers to the ability to be represented and operated on across different levels/parts of the organisation, and across different scales (both spatial and temporal). Too broad and we lose coherence, especially across operational contexts or phases in the journey; too granular and it will be hard to scale as different groups work under different contexts. Purpose, Vision and Values can be periodically revisited, but the Purpose needs to tolerate ongoing situational shifts, and designed at the right level of granularity for the system.

- **Experiment widely and learn:** When dealing with complexity, the first step is to Probe or Experiment. Most organisational transformation contexts are complex, meaning we can only understand why things happen in retrospect after we probe the system to see how the patterns settle. We have to allow the path forward to reveal itself, and the process of experimenting widely is the right probe-sense-respond (probe first, then sense, and then respond) approach for working with the complex adaptive system [20].

  Important to note is that we have to experiment widely across a portfolio of small probes (not one large experiment) so we are learning across multiple hunches and hypotheses. A portfolio approach allows us to weed out the deleterious mutations, and selectively channel energy to the adaptive and beneficial ones.

- **Creating conditions for decentralised decision making:** People who are closest to the frontline of the organisation, and whose work is most closely connected to the environment would know how best to adapt. To enable this, the team must be empowered to make decisions within its sphere of influence. This is the "empowered execution" of McChrystal's Team-of-Teams, and individualised P&L of micro-enterprises of Haier. People have to understand the sphere of their influence, and be empowered within those enabling constraints.

  If the Purpose and Strategic priorities are resonant and clear, then the organisation is working toward the same "why" and "what". The "how" can be left to those closest to the action, with appropriate guardrails in place. These guardrails will be adjusted to be specific to different teams, programs and functions.

Respond

The response capability is the system's response after experimenting with different adaptive mutations. These responses tend to either address a challenge or threat, or capitalise on an opportunity. Current trends in organisational transformations are about enhancing the speed of response, and also about effectively fulfilling the hypothesis of *value*, on which the response is based upon. Some areas for responding externally are new and modified products, partnerships and developing regenerative systems for better environmental sustainability. In rare cases a response may be to acquire another company. Internally, the system will also need to consistently adapt and respond to employee needs.

"Respond" is enhanced by:

- **Alignment to strategic priorities:** Aligning priorities involves choices about what to do now, what could be done later and what to stay away from doing. There must be alignment among the relevant stakeholders on what tradeoffs are being made when something is marked as higher priority, and the outcomes that are linked to those choices. Alignment must be achieved across the value stream, as well as supportive functions.

   Responses will have to be aligned to the priorities, as well as measures of success. We also have to ensure that priorities and success measures meet the criteria of the right level of granularity.

- **Co-creation:** Any response that requires delivering value to a stakeholder in the external ecosystem (e.g. customers, citizens), and any opportunity that needs close collaboration, (e.g. internal partnerships with employee teams, ecosystem partnerships with vendors or intermediaries), is based on the hypothesis that co-creation enhances the value being delivered and experienced. The best way to continuously validate the hypothesis is to involve the stakeholders in co-creation, as this builds continued stakeholdership into the experience or product being delivered.

   For the organisation, this also keeps the feedback cycles shorter, which enables speed of response, as well as avoiding mismatch of expectations.

- **Placing focus on genuine value delivery:** Value is the benefit delivered to the intended stakeholder, typically the customer. Whether something is valuable or not is decided by the recipient of the offering, and not the enterprise who has created and delivered the offering. Hence, in addition to getting the feedback cycles short and inviting greater co-creation to guide what value should be delivered, the validation of the hypotheses of value is critical.

In larger scale and more complicated operations where the development/production cycles are less open for rapid design and delivery, we recommend integrating thinking about marginal value, incremental delivery and product planning as not all features are created equally valuable.

For example, a product may have 20 features, of which 7 features are delivering 80% of value, at 50% of the projected cost. When these 7 features have been delivered, it is recommended to analyse whether it is worth delivering the remaining 13 features, which will deliver 20% of incremental value at 50% additional cost. Perhaps it is worth considering spending the balance 50% on another initiative that offers a greater value return.

While the incremental delivery approach works best with technology-based offerings, it can also apply to physical products and services. To help illustrate this, we borrow an example from a previous client. In this example, we are working with a car manufacturer who has launched a car targeted at young urban professionals. To appeal to the target demographic, the car has been designed to feature a sporty look, but the pricing has been kept at an entry level to enhance affordability. The car was launched with basic features; advanced features like sports suspension and infotainment system were to be launched subsequently with accompanying price increases. However, they realised after the launch that the car was more popular with the middle-aged and upper-middle-class demographic, who got the value from the sporty look without paying a premium price. This user segment was not keen to have the sports suspension and infotainment system at the incremental higher price, which disrupted the client's pricing strategy. The client recognised the need to meet their customers where they were, and reworked the features and pricing strategy instead, based on the perceived value from its customers.

The following visual depicts the marginal thinking approach when delivering value.

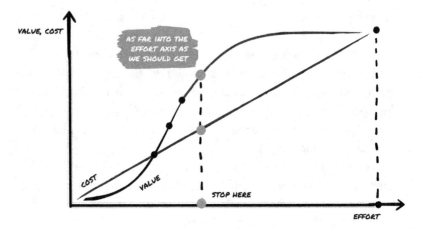

Figure 3.6 Value Delivery depicts an approach to marginal thinking when making decisions about investing resources and time for additional changes, and how to balance and trade-off against realised value from the investment.

EVOLVABILITY: THE LOOP THAT KEEPS ON LOOPING

Some organisations have now started investing in what Nicolaj Siggelkow and Christian Terwiesch from Wharton School of Business term a "Connected Strategy" [21] that enhances organisations to continuously keep that loop going. Citing the example of Disney's new *MagicBand* or *MagicMobile*[1], they illustrate the value of an on-going Sense-Adapt loop, and keeping the "respond" decision till the right moment that builds on marginal cost and value thinking.

(In the past, when you visited Disney), the connection you had with Disney was a ticket. You would hand over the ticket and enter the park, and that was the transaction that you had. Nowadays, the MagicBand allows you, as a customer, to have easy, frictionless transactions. It opens up your hotel room. It opens up the fast lane. You can easily purchase things with it. Of course, that sometimes makes also the bill rather magical at the end of the trip because you didn't even notice all you were purchasing because it was so easy to do. But from the customer perspective, it makes it a very nice experience.

What it allows Disney to do is to really know where everyone is within the park. As a result, they can direct you, for instance, to a line of an attraction that is shorter. Or you can pre-program a particular itinerary. That allows Disney to jumpstart operations at the moment they open up the gates to the park. In some senses, this is where we call it the magic of the Magic Band or the magic of the connected strategy: it makes the customer happier, while at the same time drives efficiency for the company. [22]

The Sense-Adapt-respond loop is a loop that keeps going without end. It is also multiple loops at any given point in time. Every person has their own loop, and each team will have its own; and each organisation will have its own. The speed of response and feedback depends on how fast we allow this loop to close. Organisations are trending toward pushing adaptive decisions to the frontline as this allows for the loops to be unbuffered. However, to do this, the "spine" remains critical as it provides the enabling constraints that keep the disparate initiatives coherent, and aligned to the strategic intent and purpose of an organisation.

NOTE

1 Disney's MagicMobile Service is a complimentary, contactless feature that can be activated through the My Disney Experience app. The MagicBand is a band worn on the wrist of customers that extends the MagicMobile to more contactless ease. Users use it to access the theme parks and hotel rooms, as well as to make purchases. This band allows Disney to track activity, and cater better to the user's experience.

REFERENCES

[1] Interview with Antonio Boadas, CCO GE Appliances. (31 Dec 2021) "How to apply the Rendanheyi outside of China. The GE Appliances story", in *Entrepreneurial Ecosystem Enabling Organisation*. Accessed 29 March 2023. https://stories.platformdesigntoolkit.com/howto-apply-the-rendanheyi-outside-of-china-the-ge-appliances-story-be8a049e4a2c

[2] Interview with Zhang Ruimin, CEO Haier. (27 Jul 2021) "Shattering the status quo: A conversation with Haier's Zhang Ruimin", in *McKinsey Quarterly*.

[3] Pim de Morree. (26 Sep 2018) "RenDanHeYi: The organisational model defining the Future of Work", in *Corporate Rebels: Blog*. Accessed 30 March 2023. https://www.corporate-rebels.com/blog/rendanheyi-forum

[4] Corporate Rebels. Accessed 31 March 2023. https://www.corporate-rebels.com

[5] Joost Minnaar & Pim de Morree. (2020) *Corporate Rebels: Make Work more Fun.* Corporate Rebels Nederland B.V.

[6] Dave Snowden. (Summer School 2016) "How leaders change culture through small actions", in *AcademiWales YouTube*. https://www.youtube.com/watch?v=MsLmjoAp_Dg

[7] Jim Highsmith. (14 Aug 2012) "What is agility?", in *ThoughtWorks: Blogs*. Accessed 3 Apr 2023. https://www.thoughtworks.com/en-sg/insights/blog/what-agility

[8] MIT Sloan Executive Education. (6 Apr 2021) *Webinar with Kate Isaacs: Free to Innovate - The advantage of Nimble Organizations*. YouTube. Accessed 3 April 2023. https://www.youtube.com/watch?v=U6jaw3oruHE

[9] Alvin Toffler. (1985) *The Adaptive Corporation*. McGraw-Hill.

[10] Deborah Ancona, Eliane Backman & Kate Isaacs. (Jul–Aug 2019) "Nimble Leadership: Walking the line between creativity and chaos", in *Harvard Business Review Magazine*.

[11] Deborah Ancona & Henrik Bresman. (2007) *X-Teams: How to Build Teams that Lead, Innovate and Succeed*. Harvard Business Review Press.

[12] Gen Stanley McChrystal, Tantum Collins, David Silverman & Chris Fussell. (2015) *Team of Teams: New Rules of Engagement in a Complex World*. Portfolio.

[13] EFMD Global Focus Magazine. (2022) *RenDanHeYi: Pioneering the Ecosystem Economy in the Internet of Things Era*.

[14] Mark J. Greeven, Katherine Xin & George Yip. (Mar-Apr 2023) "How Chinese companies are reinventing management", in *Harvard Business Review Magazine* (101: 2, 104–112).

[15] Charles Manz, Frank Shipper & Greg Stewart. (2009) "Everyone a team leader: Shared influence at W.L. gore associates", in *Organisational Dynamics* (38: 3, 239–244).

[16] Genetic Drift. (24 Mar 2023). "Definition taken from National Human Genome Research Institute". Accessed 3 April 2023. https://www.genome.gov/genetics-glossary/Genetic-Drift

[17] Amy Edmonson. (1999) "Psychological safety and learning behavior in work teams", in *Administrative Science Quarterly* (44: 2, 350–383).

[18] Amy Edmonson. (2018) *The Fearless Organisation: Creating Psychological Safety in the Workplace for Learning, Innovation and Growth*. Wiley.

[19] Damien Mecheri. (2019) *The Works of Fumito Ueda: A Different Perspective on Video Games*. 3rd Edition.

[20] Dave Snowden & Mary Boone. (Nov 2007) "A leader's framework for decision-making", in *Harvard Business Review Magazine* (85: 11, 68).

[21] Nicolaj Siggelkow & Christian Terwiesch. (2019) *Connected Strategy: Building Continuous Customer Relationships for Competitive Advantage*. Boson: Harvard Business Review Press.

[22] Interview with Nicolaj Siggelkow & Christian Terwiesch. (20 May 2019) "For the win: Using connected strategies to gain competitive advantage", in *Knowledge at Wharton*. Accessed 3 Mar 2024. https://knowledge.wharton.upenn.edu/article/connected-strategy-book/

Four

INTRODUCTION: SENSEMAKING GAPS AND ORGANISATIONAL DEBT

Many aspects of a society are like the meandering streets of old cities: the entrenched results of paths of activity laid down long ago for reasons no one remembers, persisting because people have grown attached to their own ways and by-ways, and the costs of tearing them up and carrying out a master plan would be too great.

—Entrenchment, by Pulitzer Prize-winner, Paul Starr

In previous chapters, we have discussed the principles that underpin, and which can guide us to design a different approach to change and transformation. These involve a strategy that is capable of continuous adaptation, with a view of enhancing overall dynamic evolvability, rather than engineering toward a specific transformed state. In this chapter, we will begin turning our attention to how to take strategy down the wall and into the lives of your people.

In genetic evolution, evolutionary scientists describe that evolvability is influenced by the dynamic interaction of the organism and its environment, and the impact this has on the organism's disposition to developing variation – our ability to respond to stresses from a rapidly changing environment [1]. Kirschner and Gerhart's landmark article on *Evolvability*, published in the Proceedings from the National Academy of Sciences in 1998, remark that systems are either **optimising** to reduce variation after repeated processes of natural selection, or **adapting** to produce variability and mutating for novel traits, or in select cases, are "frozen accidents" (because natural selection works with the best available at the time, not the best possible). Translating this into organisational speak, these states and evolutionary impulses can be observed through:

DOI: 10.4324/9781003505433-5

- Our impulse toward Optimisation: Business efforts to optimise organisational systems around selected business processes and models, and constraining systems to reduce variability so we can scale reliably and repeatably; or
- Our impulse toward Adaptation: Responses toward shifts in the environment and interacting parts of the system that are local coping responses that accumulate over time; or variability and ingenuity that find different ways (sometimes better) to get the job done. People work around the constraints present in their system to move work forward.

These evolutionary impulses are natural and work together. We need stability and to constrain variability for organisational scale. And, we also need consistent adaptation to respond to inevitable environmental perturbation. However, organisations are human systems – and human systems present complexity beyond natural impulses. Unlike genetic evolution that remains value neutral in selecting its pathways, human systems have institutional memory and cultures that cause obsolete and poor-fit systems to persist even when they reduce their evolvability.

In this chapter, we introduce the importance of shifting our understandings of scaling transformation and strategic evolution – in particular, we pay attention to how these show up in our day-to-day navigation of change through organisational memory and debt. To do this, we suggest three ways to reframe how we make sense of enacting transformation to address some fundamental gaps in our sensemaking of change.

SENSEMAKING GAP 1: REFRAMING OUR UNDERSTANDING OF "SCALE"

Moving beyond Pilots

It is very likely that most change practitioners and agents of transformation have encountered some level of success at running change interventions in selected pilots. We are all familiar with the narrative at some level: "Let's find a few select groups and spaces in the system/ organisation where we can pilot our ideas. We will use it to learn, and then we can scale". We have described this approach in Chapter 2, with the Phased and Thin Slice approaches to change. In our experience, this is one of the most common approaches.

The problem we have found is this: Pilots are very often successful.

There is a certain sense of special-ness in having been chosen for a pilot, and there is excitement and momentum that builds from that. The effort it takes to build political buy-in for a pilot also implies that those involved are motivated to create the conditions necessary to make it successful. The issue is that the pilot takes place under extraordinary conditions, and is then seen as an exemplar from which to create a module that can scale across the organisation without sufficient consideration to the different and varying contexts and conditions across the organisation.

Complex, not Complicated

This dominant framing of scale often focuses on the module of the change (what needs to be changed, and controlled components of how), and not enough on the modularity of the intervention, or contexts they have to come to life within. This approach assumes an ordered and Complicated system (see Chapter 2), and the ability to repeat, aggregate and control. Organisations, however, are complex adaptive human systems. Whilst organisations will display some coherence across the system, each department, function, local site, group and silo will present its own unique starting conditions. Very simply put, what worked in one area does not work in another. People also often resist change being done to them, and require the ability to create their own meaning around the intervention, and to make it their own.

Our sensemaking framework around scale tends to default to a product and consumer orientation – the framework is one of diffusion, which focuses on the replication of a programme, product or organisational model in multiple geographic locations and contexts to maximise the number of people that it reaches [2]. Diffusion works when there is a clear "product and consumer"; however, institutional transformation tends to also be about enacting structural and systemic changes to stimulate new ways of thinking, doing, being and organising [3] – and, in that, it falls short.

We have to reframe how we think when we consider scale. It is not a simple cut-and-paste exercise, where repeating a magic formula will bring about change. This might work in mechanical systems but not in complex human systems. You might, for example, be able to scale change in a fully automated system. Advances in technology have made it possible to automate many mechanical processes across an organisation. These tend to be manual processes, which are repetitive in nature and can be easily automated with the right set of tools and capabilities. Some recent innovations in supply chain technology with blockchain-enabled tracking chips have made inventory management much easier than before, and have helped many organisations save on time and human error. However, where there is overlap with a human element, these tend to require a different approach. In fact, in some recent experiences, what we have found is a certain amount of push-back from honour-based cultures. These groups are proud of the deep sense of implicit trust that exists between stakeholders. The implementation of an automated tracking system might appear straightforward with its promises of efficiency and savings, but required careful introduction and high-level leadership navigation so as not to compromise client-vendor relationships.

Where we are looking to impact organisational dynamics and culture, this gets even more tricky. Some recent trends toward distributing leadership (see Chapter 3) have required the cultivation of greater psychological safety in organisations. Well-intending leaders we have observed might be vocal in trying to "give" psychological safety in meetings. I have literally heard a leader in a meeting say, "Please feel free to speak up. I 'give' you psychological safety". Whilst the attitude is encouraging, this appears to betray a lack of understanding that psychological safety is an emergent aspect of how teams are used to interacting; and not something that can be explicitly given. In trying to "give" it, we are reducing it to something that can just as easily be revoked. In building a culture of psychological safety, defaulting to permission-granting works against it in the long run. To truly cultivate safety, teams need to change their patterns of interaction over a period of time. Where proper meeting and de-brief hygiene is observed, new patterns of interaction can then encourage a sense of trust and safety to emerge.

What is "Scale"?

In general, as straightforward as things might appear, the broader and more extensively we wish to achieve scaled transformation, the more we have to factor in context. This might sound antithetical to how we traditionally understand the concept of scaling because so much of management literature has been based on a concept of controlling for uniformity and repeatability.

Scale has been defined as "the adaptation, uptake and use of innovations such as practices, technologies, and... arrangements across broader communities of actors" [5], as well as with the recognition that "scale is a construction, an abstraction, a relation, a process, and a shaper of social power relations, rather than a 'thing' in itself" [4]. It is more useful to consider scale as a "temporary site" where people self-organise, and new relationships, patterns and behaviours emerge. The transformation will unfold differently for each temporary site, and people will need to be able to make sense of the changes and situate it within their own context for it to be meaningful.

To truly understand scaling in complex adaptive human systems, therefore, we turn to the science of scaling transformation in social systems for inspiration [2–6].

System thinkers from the social sciences suggest several ways to think about scale:

Table 4.1 Different Types of Scale

Scaling out	Involves stabilising, growing, replicating, transferring, spreading and speeding up [6]; or, the efforts to replicate and disseminate innovative programs, products and ideas [7]	Growth as site; breadth and spread
Scaling up	Efforts seeking to make qualitative policy changes or influencing new standards that alter the rules of the game within systems [7]	Formal system as site; conditions and constraints
Scaling deep	Structural changes that transform the quality of social relations; this occurs through changes in "people's hearts and minds, their values, and cultural practices" [3]	Agents as site; structural/power relations
Scaling down	Point to the importance of recognising when things are "non-scalable", and where localising projects, or "scaling up by scaling down" provide the best vehicle for systemic change [8]. It might also involve strategic decoupling of value streams or value chains to identify how adaptability can be developed in more strategic and selective ways.	Localisation/ interpretation or decoupling as site; mutability

Describes different ways to think of scale, as well as the sites where these forms of scaling take place.

Traditional, linear approaches to scale match more closely to the "scaling out" definition, treating scale as an absolute (i.e. this has worked, now let's make it work everywhere in the organisation). Scale is seen literally, and the site for transformation is growing the specific program of change across the organisation itself.

To understand "scale" in complex adaptive systems, we need to incorporate a careful blend of scaling up, scaling deep and scaling down. Scaling up is important to support the necessary change of conditions and constraints to enable new patterns to proliferate. Scaling deep takes a more relational approach, and recognises the importance of bringing people along. And scaling down, recognises the localisation necessary for people to conduct their own sensemaking and way-finding in order to interpret, make sense and then make the change their own. It accounts for the localised, team and interaction-level relations that connect prescription to practical reality.

Typologies of Scale

In this section, we will be building out the typologies of scale with more explanations and examples. Here, we want to clarify that our concept of scale needs to be re-imagined and reframed for non-precise human systems. Based on the traditional product-driven concept of scale, scalable projects are those that can expand without changing. This means the exclusion of conditions of diversity from scalable designs.

This, however, denies the nature of complex adaptive systems that are subject to constant emergence as well as varying conditions and changeability. "Scalability is possible only if project elements do not form transformative relationships that might change the project as elements are added. But transformative relationships are the medium for the emergence of diversity. Scalability projects banish meaningful diversity... Scalability is not an ordinary feature of nature. Making projects scalable takes a lot of work" [7]. In Anna Tsing's paper "On Non-scalability", where she describes how the living world is not really amenable to precision-nested scales, she traces the history of scalability as a concept to business.

Scalability in business is the ability of a firm to expand without changing the nature of what it does. This concept can be seen in references to things like "economies of scale" that focus on the organisational practices that make goods cheaper because more are being produced; or in technology where systems have been pixelated to scale down and up. Business scalability has been about expansion for growth and profits [7].

Even in Anthropologist, Clifford Geertz's study on markets in Java in the mid-twentieth century (1972), he expressed concern that instead of scalable firms, Javanese traders based their businesses on relationships with buyers and other traders because this meant that every time they expanded their networks, the business changed. Geertz believed that the absence of scalable firms for expansion meant that Javanese markets could not be developed [8]. However, what we are observing in today's environment is increasing uncertainty, whether due to geopolitics and access to resources that affect supply chain instability, or the rate of change of technology and disruption. This means that firms are increasingly going back to the basics of building strong relationships, or seeking new, above-brand partnerships to cultivate market share.

Scale, therefore, is due for a radical rethink. This section presents some typologies of scale that can help enterprises to approach scale in different ways.

Scaling Out

Scaling out resembles most closely our traditional product-driven approach to thinking about scale. Here, the ability to scale and grow involves the need for stabilising a product or service in a way that makes it replicable so that scale can occur by growing, replicating, transferring and spreading a product/service across a market/markets or target audience [6]. The main efforts involved in such an approach imvolve the ability to replicate and disseminate innovative programs, products and ideas [9].

There are slight differences in scaling out, however, based on how similar or different the scaling context is across the target markets or audiences. In some cases, the context across the pilot and audience at scale might be very similar, and it is easier to scale with a **direct transfer** of a program or idea. In some cases, however, there might be slight differences in context that require us to extract **main principles that can be adapted** to map into the sub-markets or sub-cultures.

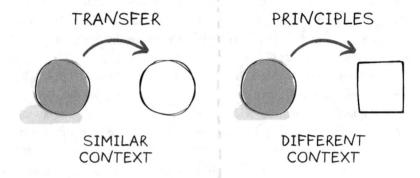

TRANSFER　　　PRINCIPLES

SIMILAR　　　　DIFFERENT
CONTEXT　　　　CONTEXT

Figure 4.1 Scaling Out by Transfer (left) depicts the ability for us to scale through a basic transfer of existing product and form, or replication where contexts are similar. **Scaling Out by Principles (right)** depicts the need for us to scale through principle rather than direct transfer when contexts are different, as it requires us to adapt the solution, whilst maintaining core principles, to suit the different context.

Scaling Out by Transfer

Google's adoption of the scale-out strategy for the Android platform can be seen as an example of scaling-out achieved through Transfer. The wide availability and adoption of the Android platform contributed tremendously to Google's success in moving into the platform and hardware market.

In this case, the scaling of the Android platform and growth of the market were achieved through a strategy that involved designing the Android platform in such a manner that enabled efficient handling of additional servers, providers and devices as the market and linked service providers adopted the platform. Rather than focus on increasing the capacity of individual components, Google focused on building a platform, and on enhancing the capacity of the platform, as well as issuing standards that promoted efficient uptake and growth of users.

The transfer supported its global reach as Android's availability was not limited to specific regions or markets. By partnering with numerous manufacturers and carriers worldwide, Google ensured that Android devices were accessible to people across the globe, contributing to the platform's massive adoption.

Alongside the development of the platform, Google also cultivated a linked app ecosystem through the Google Play Store, the primary app distribution platform for Android. It also provided monetisation strategies for developers globally, which included revenue from app sales, in-app purchases, advertisements, and services integrated into the Android ecosystem, such as Google Drive and Google Photos. This meant it was able to scale its other offerings by transferring their use on the back of Android adoption.

To facilitate the scale-up, Google also actively participated in knowledge and capacity transfer through its Android Developer program, offering tools, resources and support to encourage app development for the platform. This approach of enabling the market by making standards and how-tos explicit created a steady stream of innovative and useful apps, enhancing the overall user experience.

Scaling Out by Principle

Beyond the scaling out by transfer, Google also recognised that there are aspects of scaling a platform globally that would require adaptation. Google had developed Android as an open-source operating system. This meant that device manufacturers and the broader community could access and modify the source code. By doing so, Google encouraged collaboration, innovation and a wide range of devices from various manufacturers running on Android. This open approach attracted a large number of device manufacturers and partners.

Google also partnered with various device manufacturers like Samsung, LG, HTC, etc., to create a wide range of Android devices. This approach allowed Google to tap into the expertise of different manufacturers, enabling them to create devices that catered to various market segments, price points and regions. This strategy also helped Android gain a significant market share across different types of devices, from entry-level smartphones to high-end models.

Whilst the principles of the platform and code were kept fairly consistent across the board, they allowed for collaborative development with partners as long as core principles were maintained. This was enabled by extensive data and intelligence gathering. Device and service integration with the platform allowed for the collection of valuable user data that was used to further refine offerings, and to provide more personalised experiences. This data-driven approach improved user engagement and allowed Google to offer targeted advertising, further contributing to their revenue.

This example of Google's Android strategy illustrates a market-oriented example of transformation. This customer and market-led approach should ideally influence the organisational design and operations. For internal transformation, scaling out by direct transfer could look like utilising the exact same programs, training and messaging across the organisation, and could work for organisations that demonstrate homogeneity in specific areas. For example, a company adoption of a new brand and image should uniformly be scaled out, however, there may be principle-level adaptations to make sure that the branding can be translated into specific departments and/or sites.

Or, a new operating system being rolled out across a company could have its specifications consistently maintained across the board. However, there might be variations and adaptation to how its use and uptake is done. The company might identify a workflow management tool like Azure DevOps to maintain consistency across how teams are organising and making work visible. However, the organisation will likely allow for variation across individual teams and workgroups, particularly if they are spread across different types of work. We might need to allow for variation across different levels of granularity of tasks or work areas, and scale through principle.

Scaling Up

Scaling up is about creating the right conditions for scale to occur, specifically by seeking to make qualitative policy changes or influencing standards that alter the rules of the game within systems [9]. The metaphor of "leading like a gardener" also describes this well, as it focuses on the imperative that leaders must set the conditions for others to successfully grow and produce fruit. "The gardener cannot actually grow tomatoes, squash, or beans. She can only foster an environment in which the plants do so." In this case, we see the formal system as the site of scale, and focus on managing and advocating around conditions and constraints.

Against the backdrop of unprecedented change and deep uncertainty, many organisations are starting to adopt above-brand partnerships and strategies. The focus is therefore on strategic partnerships

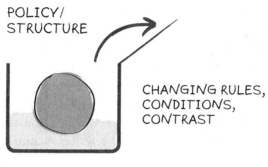

POLICY/
STRUCTURE

CHANGING RULES,
CONDITIONS,
CONTRAST

Figure 4.2 Scaling Up depicts the need to consider the policy and structures that govern or affect the contexts. This might require us to work at
the level of trying to influence a change in rules or manage the conditions
to enable scale.

that can provide an edge that allows them to influence the way the
industry evolves, rather than to be purely passive and reactive – these
are most trade associations, member organisations and standards-
establishing groups. Participation in shaping the agenda, and identifying priority areas for research and action also allow them to draw
from the resources and sensemaking of the collective.

To paint an example, we see this particularly in industries who are
experiencing a high amount of uncertainty and pressure to change,
such as in oil and gas producers, or shipping. Climate change and
the need for developing cleaner and more innovative approaches to
their business, while continuing to supply energy, and keep goods
and products moving to keep the world going exert a paradox of pressures on companies in these industries. In the words of Danny Hillis,
the founder of Applied Minds and visiting professor at the MIT Media
Lab, "empowered by the tools of the Enlightenment, connected by
networked flows of freight and fuel and finance, by information and
ideas, we are becoming something new. We are at the dawn of the
Age of Entanglement" [11].

The deep entanglement and interwoven nature of our systems mean
that change in one area often brings about many unintended and
unknowable consequences. Transformation for enterprises in these
industries have a knock-on impact that ripple into other industries, as
well as the public sector. Transformation has to be carefully charted
and managed, with plans iteratively evolving one move at a time.

To navigate into strong headwinds and centrifugal forces, we see players banding together across competitive boundaries to form associations that can help broker and create standards for member parties. The International Association of Oil and Gas Producers (IOGP) is a membership-based platform that has been around since 1974. It started as a forum for oil and gas companies to coordinate across health and safety standards to protect workers, and to create and influence a set of safety behaviour and practices that make it easy for workers and contractors to move from one facility to another without incident as coordinated standards meant everyone understood a common set of symbols and rules. The stated purpose for the IOGP is "We are the global voice of our industry, pioneering excellence in safe-efficient and sustainable energy supply - an enabling partner for a low carbon future" [12]. In 2020, the Association partnered with the American Petroleum Institute, as well as the International Petroleum Industry Environmental Conservation Association, another global oil and gas association focused on advancing environmental and social performance across the energy transition, and published Sustainability Reporting Guidance that helps provide common ways of benchmarking across member companies.

Likewise, in shipping, we see players like the Sustainable Shipping Initiative (SSI) which was founded in 2010 by Forum for the Future, World Wildlife Foundation and an ambitious group of shipping leaders: ABN Amro, BP Shipping, Gearbulk, Lloyd's Register, and Maersk Line to create "a multi-stakeholder collective of ambitious and like-minded leaders, driving change through cross-sectoral collaboration to contribute to − and thrive in − a more sustainable maritime industry" [13].

These member-based collectives provide the ability to impact transformation across a broader range of industries. Their governance structures tend to also be trustee, or board of director based, and feature membership across competitors in their industry. This structure of governance creates its own challenges such as running the risk of member lobbying for continued unsustainable practices to support shareholder interests, however, the General Committee format also creates sufficient tension such that progress is often made only when members agree to work above-brand and competitive interests. And, any standards established, or decisions made by the collective have the potential to impact on the industry's practices across the board, as well as through cross-sector influence.

Scaling up within an organisation might include reviewing structure, processes and rules to relax, tighten or change them to stimulate new patterns. Efforts at scaling up would involve changing the conditions of how people work and interact, and get things done, as well as how resources are allocated, and constraints are managed to enable better self-organisation within people and networks to bring about the type of change that responds to the new environment.

Organisations need to "scale-up" during a transformation to ensure that their structures, processes and environmental effects are shaped to enable employees to concentrate on doing the work they need to do to implement change, rather than having to consistently work around or combat friction that comes from formal systems designed to fit a previous paradigm.

Scaling Deep

Scaling deep is about hearts and minds, and takes a more relational approach. It recognises the importance of bringing people along in any attempts to change.

> Systems transformation is deeply political. Any system — whether it is a food system or the health sector — represents a locked-in constellation of structures, resource flows, relationships, and narratives. Or, as W. Edwards Deming allegedly stated: Every system is perfectly designed to get the result that it does. In any system, certain actors have privileged access and ability to shape how the system functions and how it produces outcomes. These actors will usually benefit more than others from resource flows in the system, and they are likely to oppose change.
>
> Approaches that seek to transform a system necessarily tinker with privileges and the processes that decide "who gets what, when and how" — this is the realm of power and politics. [14]

We have previously addressed resistance to change in any system as a kind of "antibody" reaction. Beyond the challenge to people's habits and comfort levels, genuine change also tends to result in a shift in access and privilege within the system. Middle managers, for example, have commonly been referred to as the permafrost of any organisation, or "the place where all good ideas go to die" [15]. In most innovative change initiatives, it seems to appear that the top management understands the importance to the business to evolve, and that those at the working level want to try new ideas. Middle managers are seen as getting in the way of change, preferring to manage according to established and known rules. They have become the convenient scapegoats for stifling change and innovation.

However, it is also important to note that "most middle managers are incentivised by their top executives to reach specific revenue and profit numbers. Their ability to deliver on these goals is the only conversation that happens at the annual review. Their bonuses and promotions depend only on their ability to execute and deliver on the core activities" [16], and transformation and change represents a disruption of, or distraction from core activities. Without reviewing internal frameworks for how we reward people, people are not being brought along. Value creation, and how value is perceived is a process of meaning and sensemaking which is a gap that change agents need to actively manage.

The hardware of systems such as processes and protocols are often the subject of conversations about transformation, particularly when

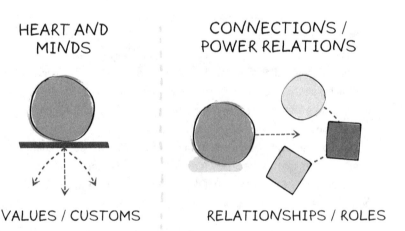

HEART AND MINDS

VALUES / CUSTOMS

CONNECTIONS / POWER RELATIONS

RELATIONSHIPS / ROLES

Figure 4.3 Scaling Deep Through Hearts and Minds (left) depicts the need to understand and get deep into influencing the values and customs of people for scale to occur. **Scaling Deep Through Connections and Power Relations (right)** depicts the need to affect relationships and roles in existing power relationships and structure to scale impact.

journeys are beginning. However, for those who work in systems innovation, there is a recognition that changing the systems' "software" – the mindsets, values and principles – is more important. This is the deeper shift that starts by putting forward a different set of assumptions, values and principles at the heart of what our organisations do [17].

Scaling deep is recognising that genuine transformation impacts on the values and customs of a system, as well as disrupting existing connections and power relations, for better or worse.

To illustrate the concept, we will use the example of Unilever's Sustainable Living Initiative. This initiative began with Unilever's recognition that the values of the market had shifted into one of more conscious consumption. The market shift aligned with the organisational desire to create a more positive impact on society and the environment by promoting sustainability. Their approach involved them reviewing their entire value and supply chain and its relationship to suppliers to understand how it was either supporting sustainable practices, or reinforcing the status quo.

Connections and Power Relations

They recognised that without proper supply chain evaluation, and mindful sourcing, they could not genuinely claim to be in support of sustainability.

Their assessment of the supply chain dynamics and connections within which they were a part influenced their decision to commit to sourcing products from organic farmers and supporting women-owned businesses. By sourcing agriculture products from organic farmers, Unilever reasoned that it would contribute to the growth of more sustainable farming practices, limiting negative environmental impacts, and promoting ecosystem biodiversity. Supporting women-owned businesses also meant they were promoting gender equality and empowerment of women, aligning with the company's social responsibility goals, and supporting yet another Sustainable Development Goal of gender equality.

This process of diversification meant that Unilever's position as a purchaser and consumer was able to create positive shifts in the power relations to privilege smaller and more quality suppliers. This ended up creating a positive externality of strengthening the resilience of their supply chain as they had effectively diversified their supplier base and reduced their dependence on a limited set of suppliers.

Hearts and Minds

Another positive side effect of their supply chain changes was that they were able to demonstrate a sincere effort at embracing responsible sourcing which led to more positive consumer sentiments toward the Unilever brand. Their efforts enhanced its reputation as a responsible corporate citizen, attracting environmentally conscious consumers and investors.

Unilever's unique position as a supplier of fast-moving consumer goods also meant that their embrace of sustainability priorities delivered more sustainable products to market, thereby making it easier for the average consumer to make more conscious choices creating a multiplier effect.

This initiative started in 2010, and was predicted to take a decade to roll out [17, 18]. Unilever has since been consistently recognised globally as a leader in strategic corporate sustainability. Former CEO, Paul Polman was clear that the transformation plan toward greater sustainability and responsibility was not meant to be treated as a "bolt-on" to the business strategy – it is the strategy [19] Organisations these days are mindful of the social reputation of their brand as it is increasingly hard to attract and retain good talent. Whilst Unilever's transformation required significant initial and continued investment, this alignment to the changing social environment also makes Unilever more attractive as a partner, employer, customer and vendor.

Scaling Down

Scaling down recognises the localisation necessary for people to conduct their own sensemaking and wayfinding to interpret, make sense and then make the change their own. It accounts for the localised, team and interaction-level relations that connect prescription to practical reality. It also reminds us to recognise when things are "non-scalable", and where localising projects, or "scaling up by scaling down" provide the best vehicle for systemic change [10].

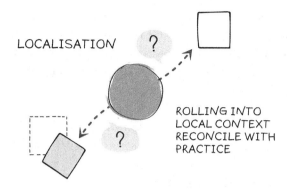

LOCALISATION

ROLLING INTO
LOCAL CONTEXT
RECONCILE WITH
PRACTICE

Figure 4.4 Scaling Down (above) depicts the need for us to allow for variability in the original idea/product/solution for it to be adapted for local context or reconciled with local practice. These will be adapted whilst retaining some fundamental principles.

John Seddon is the founder of the Vanguard Method, as well as the winner of the first Harvard Business Review/ McKinsey Management Innovation Prize for "Reinventing Leadership" in 2010 (refer to reference [20]). In his award-winning piece, he describes the importance of moving away from a "command and control" management logic to one that is driven by value delivery – with value defined by the customer, whether the customer is external or internal.

In his book, *Freedom from Command and Control* [21], he elaborates on this further by describing how initiatives in complex systems need to be scaled differently than in ordered manufacturing settings[1]. He makes a distinction here between:

- "Rolling out": Where a standardised method for improvement that has worked in one area is formulaically imposed and applied it to other areas (much like Scaling by Transfer); and
- "Rolling in": A method where change is not imposed. Instead, each area needs to learn how to do the analysis for themselves and devise their own solutions. This approach engages the workforce and produces better, more sustainable solutions.

Seddon describes that rolling out as a scaling logic tends to create problems that arise from imposed solutions that have not been optimised for each specific context, and which are then poor fits. The fact that people in other units or parts of the organisation have not gone through the learning process from which the solution had been developed creates little sense of ownership. The change is imposed, which might trigger a sense of a loss of control and/or resistance.

Seddon, therefore, recommends scale to allow for variation within purpose. The transformation should begin with a sense of purpose, whilst allowing for different groups to make sense and re-interpret the specific change in a manner that reconciles it with their under-standing of purpose for the change, and purpose of their roles within the broader organisation and value chain.

An industry example would be the need for localised customer service centres to cater to the language and cultural nuances of each locale, rather than relying solely on large centralised service centres. Whilst the service centres serve the same purpose, generally share the same script and support similar processes and systems, some varia-tions need to be accounted for to respond to different customer pro-files and needs, overlays of local regulation and protocols as well as linguistic profiles. It is more effective for a large multinational to allow for variation across its global offices within a threshold of variation.

In other cases of scaling down, organisations might also need to strategically decouple aspects of their value chain to optimise for businesses in different markets. For example, as companies in large manufacturing centres like Shenzhen have realised, the ability for the ecosystem to couple and assemble across tens, hundreds or thou-sands of components, whilst remaining agile enough to respond to customer demands for different materials and wide fluctuations in demand within a short timespan mean that large companies benefit from smaller players fitting themselves into larger production lines. In tandem, large production line companies create modularity that allow for value chain optimization that borrows from micro-specialisations in other players [22]. Strategic decoupling and modularisation allow value chains to be optimised for adaptability.

Main Take-aways

To quote Dave Snowden, "you don't scale a complex system by aggre-gation and imitation. You scale it by decomposition and recombina-tion". Amazon, for example, is a company that has successfully scaled its business by decomposing complex problems into smaller, more manageable components. Its e-commerce platform is a complex system that involves millions of products, customers, and transactions. However, by decomposing this system into smaller components, such as product listings, customer accounts and shopping cart functionality, Amazon has been able to scale its platform to handle billions of transactions per day.

Amazon also uses recombination to scale its business. Its Amazon's Web Services (AWS) platform is a collection of cloud computing services that are built on top of its own infrastructure. AWS allows developers to build and deploy applications without having to worry about the underlying infrastructure. This has led to the development of a wide range of innovative applications that are powered by AWS.

However, whilst scale is impressive, it is also critical for us to remember that some things don't have to scale. And, some things will scale through scaling down – by allowing for a process of self-selection and emergence across the system. It is also important as well to recognise that approaches to scaling require us to scale out, up, deep and down to achieve meaningful transformation. We need to identify what type of scale the situation calls for and apply our efforts across in contextually appropriate manners. Some scales are also nested, and require a variety of approaches.

- Identify first what kind of system change we are dealing with before we go ahead to invest in creating complicated standards and unnecessary controls for scaling change. Where the change is complicated, or where a product-driven approach of diffusion is suitable, creating processes and controls for scale will make sense and support standardisation. However, where things fall into the complex domain, it is difficult to "engineer" and "standardise".
- Utilising pilots to test ideas is useful, but it is often difficult to build a plan for scale around pilots owing to the issue with the exceptions that pilots typically represent. The way things unfolded for a pilot presents a low likelihood of repeating in the same way.
- Identify the conditions and constraints we need to manage to support the emergence of favourable patterns. Understand that the system is relational and that we need people to want to come along; and also recognise where we need to "scale up by scaling down", and prioritise localisation and self-organising emergence.

SENSEMAKING GAP 2: REMEMBERING TO FORGET

There is a goddess of Memory, Mnemosyne; but none of Forgetting.
Yet there should be, as they are twin sisters, twin powers, and walk on
either side of us, disputing for sovereignty over us and who we are, all
the way until death. [23]

— Richard Holmes

Institutional memory and culture are powerful tools that enable the
development of better capabilities over time and learnt experience.

Organisational memory can be understood as "stored information
from an organisation's history that can be brought to bear on present
decisions" [24]. Such a definition, however, indicates static knowledge
storage. It implies that history is merely stored and can be easily reap-
plied, even when we know that knowledge can decay or become unfit
for changing landscapes.

There needs to be active ways of sensemaking and coding past experiences to orient them to the present and future. It bears repeating that
organisations, despite the mechanical sophistication that can be observed
in some operations, remain human systems. Human systems have a bias
toward meaning. Here, the limits of the biological metaphor of organism-
level evolution become evident. Organism-level evolution is focused on
unbiased optimising to shifting conditions. Organisations, however, are
made out of people who have hopes, fears, biases, bureaucracy and management layers, and do not optimise in the same way. Organisations need
to actively address debt – both organisational debt and sensemaking debt
that tend to co-occur – in order to improve its evolvability.

Organisational Debt

The term "organisational debt" was coined by Steve Blank, and was
originally used to describe "all the people/culture compromises made
to 'just get it done' in the early stages of startup". He had compared it
to "technical debt" which refers to an accumulation of old code and
short-term solutions for a digital product that if left unpaid, collectively accrues into performance burden. Much like traditional debt, it
has to be paid back – either in a proper refactoring, or with a lot of
time, pain and money.

"Organisational debt is like technical debt - but worse" [25], as
oftentimes the debt is ignored, unacknowledged or worked around

Evolvability in Business

until it is too late. In his original Forbes article, Blank describes the types of challenges he typically saw with start-ups growing from the initial "Ideation and Development" stage into a "Build and Grow" stage. The basic idea is that start-ups tend to focus on speed at the beginning since they are burning cash everyday as they search for product/market fit. They are agile and able to shift strategies quickly especially in their early stages. Oftentimes, they accomplish this by compromising on features and many aspects of their organisation design. If the product is successful and the company grows, however, the scale of the organisational debt can quickly become problematic.

Founders tend to be motivated about maintaining their growth, and this is typically driven by an increase in headcount. As the organisation grows, as does its structural and processual needs. Funding stages and investors, however, tend to be focused on targets and valuation, and this dominates the thinking rather than the very real issues of change and transformation at the organisational level that are needed to support the people on whom the early stage was built on. Some questions that need to be answered are, "So what's the training and onboarding plan for the new hires? What are you doing about the pay scales at the bottom of the organisation? Aren't you concerned about losing qualified people that the company spent the last few years training but never compensated adequately?" Most start-ups, however, tend to be reactive in these departments, rather than pro-active in addressing these challenges.

Organisational Debt and Organisational Transformation

Whereas Blank's work started from observing the patterns of compromises that start-ups made, Aaron Dignan, Founder of The Ready and Author of *Brave New Work*, developed the conversation from the organisational debt of start-ups to the debt that most organisations incur with the consistent changes in the business environment, and the need for constant adaptation. Dignan defines organisational debt as "the interest companies pay when their structure and policies stay fixed and/or accumulate as the world changes". The interest typically comes in the form of "reduced speed, capacity, engagement, flexibility, and innovation that ultimately undermine the macro objectives of the firm: to survive, thrive, and achieve its purpose" [26].

Some areas where you might be able to identify and recognise symptoms of organisational debt are.

Prioritising Short-term Objectives

Pressure to achieve certain financial targets, or to meet unrealistic deadlines can influence people to prioritise short-term objectives at the expense of long-term impact. Some classic examples are decisions to cut back on expenses related to employee well-being to manage costs and improve the balance sheet, at the expense of the negative impact it might have on employee morale. Or, in the case of technology products, meeting an unrealistic deadline can come at the cost of suboptimal architecture and design, which can create technical debt.

Realistic targets and timelines are important, as well as understanding that genuine transformation takes time. When short-term objectives are prioritised over time, these accumulate to compromise on the broader transformation, and also create a culture of short-sightedness in decision-making.

Process – Too Much and Too Little

Workarounds your process are a great indicator of how relevant and up-to-date a process is for the work as it evolves. Employees usually employ workarounds when they believe that following a process is inefficient and/or is not helping to achieve intended outcomes.

Understanding the workarounds – which often involve shortcuts that improve flow of work – may help with updating and optimising the process, However, we have to maintain balance between optimising something locally, as well as understanding how optimisation in one area might have consequences on the broader value stream. In this sense, process can help or hinder, and requires us to recognise the need to review and renew as needed.

Not removing processes that have become obsolete add to organisational debt, as they create delays, inefficiencies and wastage in the system. For example, maintaining manual physical records for processes that have been digitised and automated might be duplicating work. However, where work is in more early stages of exploration, and more complex in nature, putting too much process in these early stages might be constraining discovery.

Structure and Empowerment

Whether the issue is too much silo-ed working, excessive centralisation of capabilities and decision-making, or a frozen middle-management layer, organisational communication and information flow tend to settle into a structure that reflects how things have been working. As we update the vision and working arrangements of teams and groups, we have to address the way teams are structured, and how people are empowered to support new ways of working. For example, in Chapter 3 we discussed two different organisational design approaches: Team-of-teams and Micro-enterprises.

In these examples, the organisations had to change not just the way people were organised and how things were structured, there was also a need to actively empower individuals in the system to make decisions and act at their level in order to make the new structure work. Without the empowerment, a structure change is akin to shifting the deck chairs on the Titanic.

To further illustrate, to maximise the effective deployment of expertise, many organisations have created internal Centres of Excellence. This allows them to deploy high-value experts who can focus on continuously learning and developing the organisational capability in a specific subject matter. Centralisation, however, creates dependencies that leads to delays. People in a centralised unit are often out of touch with the ground realities and detached from business outcomes, and where deployed, these subject matter experts lack context to make appropriate diagnosis and recommendations. An example would be the Compliance function of most large organisations. Compliance tends to define success as following regulation. They tend to have no skin-in-the-game, and are disconnected from business outcomes. They also possess the power to stall something that they believe might trigger regulation. Whilst adherence to laws and regulations are critical, not having "skin in the game" means they are less motivated to find creative solutions that might move a business decision forward.

We have outlined some examples of how organisational debt might manifest in organisations. In all cases, debt typically manifests in two ways that impact the organisation:

1. **Obsolescence:** This essentially happens when structures and policies become "unfit" for market conditions.
2. **Accumulation**: This happens when policies and procedures are constantly added but never removed.

We have spent most of the book discussing the need for transformation, and the need to update structure and policies toward becoming evolvable. In this section, we focus on debt by Accumulation rather than Obsolescence. In Chapter 2, we briefly touched on the work of Fumito Ueda, an award-winning designer, who described our tendency when seeking to improve and enhance things, to design by addition. Our change and transformation journeys tend to be led by things we need to start doing differently, but not enough by what we need to stop. This means any changes we implement consistently creates debt we have to maintain.

Ueda champions an approach of "Design by Subtraction", which encourages people to remove superfluous and extraneous parts in order to strengthen the core elements [27]. We have to be mindful of the "competing commitments" that bring about a system's immunity to change (see Chapter 2), and that we are consistently refining, and not simply adding to our system. We need to remember to help the system along by refactoring an organisation's learnt experience and memory. The title in this section is deliberately trite. It is not possible for a system to forget completely; however, we can support coherence of the new trajectory with the memory and past.

Joint Sense-making and Co-developing the Next Trajectory

Sensemaking is a generic phrase that refers to processes of interpretation and meaning production whereby individuals and groups interpret and reflect on phenomena. Through processes of sensemaking people enact (create) their world and their understanding, as well as their orientation in it [28, 29]. In traditional planned change, leaders do the sensemaking and communicate it. In complex adaptive systems, however, sensemaking has to be jointly conducted with people in the system.

Traditional management is plagued by a false thinker-doer separation. This management-worker disconnect separates the making of decisions, and the execution of them. This separation is a relic from Taylorism, and might work for highly automated and complicated systems, but is not suitable for complex knowledge work, or team/organisational dynamics.

The thinker-doer separation causes management to engage in sensegiving, which comprises narratives that explain what is going on against the background of relevant alternatives and appropriate discourses that guide how employees form their expectations. Sensegiving is an attempt to reframe sensemaking processes inline with the intended new directions [30]. Whereas it is important for management to provide the starting direction, there is a need for generative forums, discussions and feedback loops which provide people the opportunity to speak back and actively sense-make on their own, and in dialogue with the system.

Developing more participatory governance across the organisation, as well as collaboratively developing an organisational backlog to support the transformation is necessary. The system also needs to distribute leadership to encourage agency in participation and driving initiatives as this cultivates accountability for the change, and encourages continuous improvement and experimentation.

The Three Horizons Framework

As new initiatives and practices emerge and are introduced, it is important to learn to sunset obsolete practices – to actively subtract and not just accumulate.

Here, we borrow a framework from Futures Studies that helps us see across multiple horizons. The framework describes and encourages a rotation of three key perspectives as we navigate the change [29]. "The Three Horizons model was adapted significantly by the consultant Bill Sharpe, working with Anthony Hodgson, for the UK Government Foresight project on Intelligent Infrastructure systems. The specific question it was used to address was how to develop a technology roadmap over a long period (50 years), where particular technologies could not be described but their likely characteristics could be identified, or at least anticipated" [31–34].

The three horizons framework represents a useful sensemaking framework for managing a system in transition. As with most sensemaking methods, it recognises the importance of looking at the world in patterns, and how these patterns map to produce the system, but also where patterns are being disrupted and new patterns can be possible. "Three Horizons practice uses a simple framework that can easily be communicated in a few minutes. This framework includes three lines, with each line representing a system or pattern in the way things are done in a particular area of interest (e.g. how an organization operates, particular values in society, or the use of certain forms of technology). The horizontal axis represents time stretching into the future from the present, and the vertical axis indicates the prevalence of each pattern in a relative way" [34]. The framework represents three different patterns: an established first horizon pattern giving way over time to an emerging second horizon, via transitional activity in the third horizon.

1st Horizon: Viable Future – Visionary

The 1st horizon is something we are all familiar with – here we identify where we see pockets of the future embedded in the present, and where the organisation is already successfully adapting to the needs of the evolving environment. We might describe the fundamental transformations that we anticipate, and are envisioning as we nudge toward the future. To successfully navigate the sensemaking on this horizon, we pay attention to broader social, ecological, economic, cultural and technological trends and activities that may represent "pockets of this future" in the present, and which help us to understand how the organisation needs to transform to meet the future [31]. Sharpe describes this as a perspective akin to that of a Visionary persona.

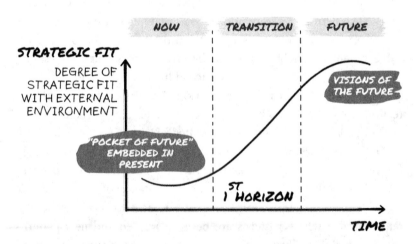

Figure 4.5 1st Horizon depicts the visionary horizon where we identify the vision of the future and also where we see pockets of the future embedded in the present, and where the organisation is already successfully adapting to the needs of the evolving environment.

This is part of our strategy process when we scan the broader market and patterns to understand how the organisation needs to adapt to meet the new challenge, as well as how we envision and plan for transformation journeys. We have to recognise, however, that this vision of the future remains a projection based on what we can know now, and that change is a process of evolution. We have to continuously learn and adapt to changing conditions. We recognise that the vision sets a direction, rather than a destination, and that moving towards this horizon always entails acknowledging that much is now known, and unknowable, and will emerge as a part of our process. To echo the title of Chapter 2, there is our roadmap, and then there is what really happens.

2nd Horizon: Business-as-usual – Manager

The second horizon focuses on identifying the parts of the system that are what is referred to as "sustaining innovation" that help to keep business-as-usual going. These help to "keep the lights on" as the organisation navigates parts of the system that are already obsolete and which need to be phased out progressively. Sharpe describes this perspective as akin to inhabiting the persona of a manager. This horizon represents the patterns of the organisation that we all reproduce

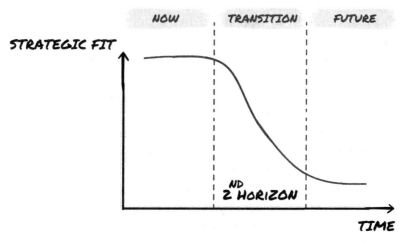

Figure 4.6 2nd Horizon depicts the sustaining practices and innovation that represent activities that can keep the lights on" as the organisation navigates forward, and progressively phases out obsolete practices.

by taking part in it, and the manager recognises the patterns that are sticky when they are not the best fit for the future.

We recognise that the current prevailing system is losing its "fit" over time as the external environment changes, but some aspects are also helping to provide vital services without which we would face organisational collapse. Transformation has to occur while these services continue to be provided and some valuable aspects will also be retained into the future so we do not run the risk of "throwing the baby out with the bath water".

This horizon tends to be the most overlooked one in transformation journeys as the focus tends to be on adding new or different ways of doing things, or systems on top of the existing. However, resistance tends to arise from an unwillingness to let go. To illustrate with a simple example would be a client we have worked with that produces software for specialty measurement instruments in high-end scientific and analytical laboratory equipment. Their work is very sophisticated, and specialised in nature, often requiring PhD holders in biology and chemistry to code the software tools that are deployed onto their equipment. Their end clients tend to be pharmaceutical companies and high-end laboratories conducting experiments in areas like aeronautics or space exploration. As a result of the deep specialisation of the work, each of their customers developed very specific requirements that led to the company having to run multiple legacy systems in parallel in order to support the diversity of specialised functions, even whilst introducing new applications.

The profit margins of the company had flatlined for many years, and in seeking to improve the margins, the company attempted transformation to streamline and reorganise their company along verticals and associated value chains.

As they navigated the transformation, the change team introduced new reporting structures, new teams and new ways of doing things. Growing the customer base also meant additional new systems to develop and maintain. However, through this journey, there was leadership reluctance to sunset legacy systems. Teams were developing new tools along the new operational verticals, whilst struggling to maintain horizontally integrated legacy systems, and patching them manually for deployment. The result was high employee burn-out and a 30% attrition rate, which was much higher than their industry standard of about 10% per annum. The intervention required leadership and teams to agree on an obsolescence timeline for legacy systems, and leadership demonstrating commitment to this by firmly communicating a timeline to their clients.

3rd Horizon: World in Transition – Entrepreneur

Now, just as visions are not implemented overnight, and change requires removing old practices, transformation is an-going journey. The 3rd horizon describes this by representing an integrative horizon. The 3rd horizon emerges as the organisation navigates the other two. In this space, we will often hear the voice of the entrepreneurial persona that sees the possibility for something different, and who recognises it is not-as-strategic a fit compared to business-as-usual, but as a way to integrate the vision of the future with the managerial concerns of today. This is an intermediate space in which the first and third horizons collide, and requires entrepreneurial and culturally creative approaches that incorporate already feasible technological, economics and cultural innovations that can disrupt and transform business-as-usual to varying degrees [29].

The space of transition is typically unstable. It is characterised by clashes of values in which competing alternative paths to the future

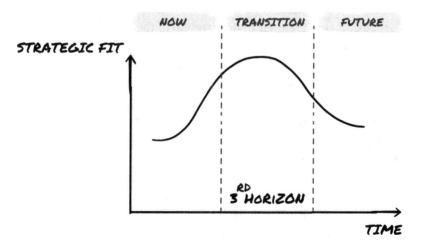

Figure 4.7 3rd Horizon depicts the transitional practices which help organisations to integrate between the vision of the future and the past.

are proposed by actors. Most of the actual work of implementing transformation occurs on this horizon, and requires us to consistently identify viable opportunities to change the scope of what is deemed possible and acceptable in an organisation. In charting a path to the future, we need to value the bridge that certain types of disruptive innovation offer. This horizon is therefore about building stepping stones rather than guaranteeing outcomes, and about experimentation with the knowledge that many initiatives will fail, but will offer valuable opportunities for learning and evolution.

All Three Horizons: An Example in Energy Transition

The Three Horizons framework recognises as we navigate a transformation, that all horizons are present in any given moment. For example, in utilising the approach, a key step would be to identify examples of how the visionary horizon is manifesting as pockets of the future in the present, and to consider how this new pattern can emerge through the 3rd "world in transition" horizon. It helps participants situate the present moment in relation to the future, and make sense of what it means for them. Each horizon is a quality of the future in the present, and characterises a distinct way of acting in the present in relation to current and future patterns. The framework is typically implemented as a "facilitated process with a diverse group of stakeholders to map out how different patterns change over time. It is the experience of being involved in the process that helps participants reframe their understanding of the relationship between the present and the future" [29], a critical step in closing the sensemaking gap that helps reframe organisational memory to make it relevant for the present.

It is helpful in each transformation to have voices who are dedicated to advocating across all of the multiple horizons so we are introducing change and new practices, whilst simultaneously learning to sunset obsolete parts of the system [32–34].

The process of transformation is one of on-going sensemaking and negotiation across the agents and the system.

The market and environment often exert landscape pressures on organisations that motivate their transformation journeys. Here, we will use the example of energy security as we transition from fossil fuels to new energies, also discussed in Andrew Curry and Anthony

Hodgson's piece that connects the Three Horizons to a transformation strategy [33, 35].

In this example, the environmental and market pressures that are forming the landscape pressure for a clean energy transition form the 1st horizon. The vision for many energy suppliers and companies is to live on energy income which is primarily powered from renewable sources, and having the hard and soft infrastructure that can support this for their customers at scale. This requires a mix of macro and micro-system changes.

The 2nd horizon is represented by the need to sunset current hydrocarbon-dependent energy income. However, to successfully navigate this, it would not be a total abandonment of business-as-usual, but to identify ways to innovatively repurpose existing infra-structure, and optimise the value chain to adapt them for renewable energy income.

The integrative 3rd horizon recognises that to navigate this, we need experimentation to include testing emerging technologies, part-nering across possible alternative social institutions, and different business models.

Let's scale this down fractally into individual energy companies. Whilst the business of carbon-based energy has gone largely unchal-lenged for the past 100 years, and has managed to achieve success with longer-horizon thinking and investments, what we observe is now a trend toward these traditional engineering companies imple-menting transformations that nudge their operations and decision-making into more agile practices with faster feedback loops, as well as early-stage venture capital-type investments that allow for portfolio-based approaches to managing risks and uncertainty.

However, as the nature of this particular change is deeply uncertain, transformational and arguably existential, not just for the companies but for general existence, this change is fraught with necessarily incom-plete information, and involves managing complexities of trade-offs. Investing in energy infrastructure is a large capital investment that often cannot see profits till decades after the decisions are made. The way we make trade-offs, and how risks and investments are weighed are "deeply informed by values. It fumbles towards utopia, using the only tools which its marginalised advocates have to hand; the power of voice and experiment" [31].

Active dialogue and sensemaking is required across the company, from leadership setting clear expectations, to those on the exploratory frontlines providing critical insight back to inform emerging frameworks and to guide how investment decisions get made. The whole system needs to be in communication: Transformation requires some high level scaffolding for consistency, whilst acknowledging that experiments will reveal new information that will require us to adapt the frameworks we began with. "In the case of energy, there are clear conflicts... around green and clean, between local and centralised, between maintaining consumption and reducing it, between self-contained energy systems and energy systems which are integrated with other social and environmental processes" [33].

Whilst this example has focused on the energy transition, and some of the deeper reframing and sensemaking needed to fumble our way forward, this framework can be applied for all transformation efforts as all organisational change triggers a need to sensemake across these three time horizons, and to identify and reconcile the conflicts across the three.

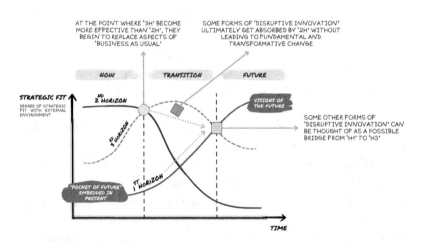

Figure 4.8 Triangle of Change depicts the tensions and dynamics between all three horizons as they occur concurrently. The triangle helps us to understand where change and action is possible; whilst recognising that this change requires experimentation to disrupt our old paradigm, and that many of these experiments might be absorbed without always leading to the types of change we are seeking.

The Triangle of Change
One of the most interesting aspects of the Three Horizons technique, which has become clear only through use, is that the shape of the curves of the different horizons effectively defines a triangle of choice, in the space where the (2nd horizon) has started to fall away, the (3rd horizon) is close to its apex, and the (1st horizon) is still gaining influence. These choices, obviously, are about the resolution of the conflicts identified (in the transition space). It is also possible to assess how these might be resolved, and which actors will capture the future social or commercial value. In most of the work done to date, such choices have typically been around strategy or policy issues. But they could equally be about choices in values. The question in this latter case becomes a question about the way in which we need to reframe discourse to enable the (visionary horizon) to emerge. [31]

The triangle not only helps us to recognise where change and action is possible, but also to recognise that this change requires disruptive experimentation to disrupt our old paradigm, and that many of these experiments might be absorbed without leading to the types of change we are seeking. Whilst the actions in the 3rd horizon introduce our visions of the future in a manner that provides more strategic fit than where we are today, they are presenting alternatives that are less of a strategic fit than the dominant 2nd horizon. The transformation is about allowing for multiple combinations of ideas, and encouraging evolvability, and not fixating on the outcome.

We have been using the energy transition as an example to illustrate the three horizons. To further elucidate, for a company in the energy sector, the three horizon model could be as follows:

1st Horizon

- **Vision:** Widespread adoption of renewable energy sources, decentralised and integrated
- **Examples:**
  - **Large-scale solar and wind farms:** Dominate energy generation, with advanced storage solutions balancing supply and demand.
  - **Microgrids:** Communities and individuals generate and manage their own energy.

- **Smart grids:** AI-powered systems which optimise energy distribution and consumption in real-time, balancing supply and demand across the network.

2nd Horizon

- **Manage through:** Optimising existing infrastructure and revenue streams while transitioning towards renewables.
- **Examples:**
  - **Carbon capture, utilisation and storage (CCUS):** Extending the life of existing fossil fuel infrastructure while reducing emissions.
  - **Renewable energy integration into existing grids:** Upgrading grids to handle multiple renewable energy sources.
  - **Efficiency improvements:** Reducing energy consumption through new technologies and behaviour changes.

3rd Horizon

- **Transitional tactics:** Experimenting with disruptive innovations that could fundamentally change the energy landscape.

Examples:

- **Peer-to-peer energy trading:** Individuals and communities directly buying and selling energy from each other.
- **Blockchain-enabled energy management:** Secure and transparent tracking and trading of renewable energy.
- **Developing new materials and technologies:** Breakthroughs in solar cells, batteries.

These three horizons will take place concurrently. The "triangle of change" will occur when the experimental tactics in the 3rd horizon become more effective than the 2nd horizon practices that are in decline. At such time, they will slowly begin to replace what has been accepted as business-as-usual. Some of the experimental practices will gain prominence, whilst others will become absorbed, and as technology and know-how improves, new radical innovation will be introduced from the 1st horizon to further speed up change. These radical innovations might not have been thought of as viable until the inflection point where the 1st horizon overtakes the 3rd.

Seeing in horizons encourages the understanding that we are managing multiple conflicting tensions in the system. We need to continuously make sense of the change, and reconcile it with organisational memory to update it for the current challenge. Organisations need to be mindful to engage in active sensemaking to help people interpret the desired change with their established practice, as well as to reconcile it with their day-to-day lives. Agents in the system need to be able to identify the micro-practices in their working areas that they can adapt for the new horizon.

In this chapter, we discuss the Three Horizons Framework as one way to scaffold the conversation – at the heart of it, it is less about frameworks, and more about the process of engaging and sensemaking, and for each group to situate the change in actions that are in their realm of agency. The goal is for organisations to create a dynamic socio-cultural environment that is conducive for transformation.

Main Take-aways

- As we introduce change and seek to bring about transformation, the organisation will start to shift and adapt. This will create organisational debt that requires us to be proactive in adjusting to ensure the interest of the debt does not accumulate. Whilst most changes tend to be additive in nature, we also need to remember to remove outdated practices and systems so they do not create "competing commitments" that bring about a system's immunity to change, and that we are consistently refining, and not simply adding to our system.

- We need to remember to help the system along by refactoring an organisation's learnt experience and memory, and to bring people along in the sensemaking. It is not sufficient for management or leadership to decide on change and to communicate top-down. There needs to be an opportunity for people to co-develop the way forward in a manner that is coherent for their own journey. The impulse is typically to sense-give, but we have to remember to allow for interactive sensemaking and collaborative way finding.

- Recognise the importance of multiple perspectives, and seeing across different horizons. It is useful to create a system of rotating these perspectives across the organisation and allowing the space of transition to emerge as a result of the tension between our impulse to adapt and our impulse to optimise – our result to introduce new ways of working and sunset old ways.

SENSEMAKING GAP 3: MONITOR WHAT'S MEANINGFUL: MIND YOUR "DEAD BODY COUNT"

After a successful stint at Ford, turning the business around with a data analysis and metric-driven approach, Robert McNamara was appointed the US Secretary of Defense during the Vietnam War.

McNamara believed he could apply similar mathematical models to war analysis. He is responsible for developing the "dead body count" metric as a key indicator of which side was winning the war. He turned a blind eye to the actual dynamics of the war situation, such as the spirit of the people fighting the war, their resistance and guerrilla warfare, feelings of the rural Vietnamese people, and the local forest conditions. "The problem was, data that were hard to quantify tended to be overlooked, and there was no way to measure intangibles like motivation, hope, resentment, or courage" [36]. For a long time, the "dead body count" was used to convey to Americans that the USA was winning the war, although the ground reality in Vietnam was entirely different.

"Uncertain how to evaluate results in a war without battle lines, the military tried to gauge its progress with quantitative measurements," he wrote in his 1995 memoir, In Retrospect [36].

Many years have passed but this thinking continues to haunt us. In many ways, trying to manage and enact transformation and change in a complex adaptive environment is much like a "war without battle lines". Daniel Yankelovich, a sociologist, coined the phrase "The McNamara Fallacy" to describe tendencies to rely heavily on metrics and numbers to draw conclusions; and ignoring the ground-level realities [37].

As outcome-focused organisations following good practice, we are also mindful to identify the outcome indicators that we will use to measure how well we are doing on our change journeys, and to check if we are creating the impact we want. From the perspective of governance, good metrics and indicators serve multiple purposes including tracking progress, allocation capacity and resources, making projections and influencing behaviours. They are useful and can provide meaningful insights and guidance for action. However, relying on metrics which are inappropriate can lead to suboptimal or wrong decisions which can cost the organisation dearly and also accumulate huge organisational debt.

Good Outcomes, Not Prescriptive Outcomes

Some issues with outcome indicators is that they are often lagging in terms of change interventions — that is, the results take time to show up. Interventions often require some training or capacity building, or change in process which requires a period of adjustment. Depending on the scale of the intervention, the business outcomes typically identified also tend to follow predetermined customer or employee feedback, or sales cycles. For example, many organisations undertake investments in change that are guided by the very sound desire to improve customer satisfaction. However, customer satisfaction is usually a composite indicator that might involve anything from a reduction in complaints to customer loyalty and renewal. Customer complaints, for example, might not necessarily drop, but shift from one topic to another, and require more nuance to be meaningful as an indicator. And, renewal or retention rates follow specific cycles that take time to show up.

Satisfaction level as an arbitrary metric also does not provide sufficient actionable insight into what variables are influencing the metric. Customer satisfaction can be impacted by product or service quality, user experience, response time, call centre experience and many more. Changes to these different aspects of the customer experience will also likely not be uniformly implemented, and customer satisfaction as a composite indicator will be impacted in varying ways by the uneven roll-in and roll-out of initiatives. Identifying these different variables could provide more leading indicators that can identify how changes are impacting on the aspects that influence the stated outcome.

Unintended Consequences: What do Cobras and Opium have in Common?

Here, however, we need to start treading with caution as any intervention in a complex adaptive system also tends to have unintended consequences. A metric set for optimising a single variable can often lead to unwanted behaviours in other areas. In Colonial British India, this took the form of cobras: During this period, there was an overpopulation of cobras in India, and there were a high number of accidents resulting from interactions with the potent snake. The British wanted to help manage this, and therefore came up with the great idea of offering a cash reward for every cobra head that was brought in by locals. This scheme worked really well at curbing the cobra population until some enterprising Indians realised that there was more money to be made from breeding cobras than killing them. Now, you would think that from all the advancements and popularisation of behavioural science that we would have learnt and know better now. However, not so long ago, we saw the same patterns repeating in Afghanistan.

Opium cultivation has a deep and complex political economy in Afghanistan. Most local farmers feed their families off the proceeds of the poppies, and "the Pentagon's Defense Intelligence Agency estimates annual Taliban revenue from drugs at about $70 million a year. Outsiders... have put the figure as high as $500 million a year. In 2008, the UNODC estimated that the Taliban and militant offshoots collected $400 million in taxes and protection payments from the drug trade" [38]. The opium trade alone is sufficient for funding the insurgency forces. When the USA occupied Afghanistan, they saw the eradication of opium as a good way to starve the Taliban off its funding. The US military reported success in undermining Taliban financing after it paid Afghan farmers to destroy their crops of opium poppies. What went unreported, however, was that the farmers had planted larger fields of opium poppies, in the hopes that they might be paid by the US military to destroy the crops again. When US payments didn't come through, the poppies were harvested and entered the international drug trade. This led to the further alienation of the American cause from the local Afghani farmers, and much of the profits from this also went on to support the Taliban's anti-American military operations [39–41].

Now, let's time-travel and context-switch into a modern call centre environment. Many call centres tend to measure and manage average call time as a key indicator for performance. If the goal is to minimise and control for average call duration, what behaviour does this incentivise, and what are potential unintended consequences? Call centre executives tend to rush through the calls or even cut the calls short abruptly to meet their KPIs. This often leads to some less-than-satisfied customers, an increase in the volume of calls if customer issues remain unresolved from the earlier call, but great performance metrics on average call time!

This is what we refer to as a "watermelon metric". Watermelons are green on the outside. However, when you cut into one, you realise that it quickly reveals red and juicy flesh. Some metrics present like watermelons – they look "green" from the outside but are actually "red" on the inside. Another example is when cost competitiveness is seen as the ultimate bottomline. This might lead to cutting back on essential expenses such as marketing, or fair pay for enthusiastic but overworked teams, which may be detrimental in the long run, or be seen in the negative effects on another indicator. In Chapter 3, we discussed the importance of nesting initiatives – indicators need to also be nested and meaningfully coupled into bodies of indicators. Oftentimes, the coupling might also surprise you as they might appear unrelated at the time.

Leading, Process and Outcome Indicators

Any change or transformation will require a process that allows for some period of socialisation of the new approach, adjustment of practices, and sensemaking to create coherence within the organisational memory. Indicators and metrics have to be considered in a body that captures the leading indicators of change, processual adjustments and then only arrive at some outcomes sometime down the line.

In recent years, adoption of Agile ways of working has been one of the most common transformation journeys we have observed. Any framework, whether it is Agile or otherwise, is essentially a set of guidelines, which needs to be customised to adapt to the context. In complex systems, every instance is different from the other, just as no human being is exactly similar to another. The same principle applies to organisations as well.

The expected outcomes of an Agile transformation are more frequent deliverables that are in touch with the concept of customer value. These, however, do not show up immediately after the first couple of sprints. Typically the first things we observe changing are the quality of conversations and discussions that teams have – the new way of working provides a scaffold that stimulates a different kind of conversation and decision-making. The habits of process are not yet adopted at an early stage. Some early-stage discussions might reveal that specific information links in the organisation are broken, and this might stimulate the development of new relationships, and processes or rituals set up to support better exchange of information and value across them. There will then be an observable process-level adjustment. Outcomes will follow only after the quality of discussions and decision-making improve, and catalyse new relationships and processes.

We, therefore, recommend that organisations put in place not just Outcome indicators for their transformation journeys, but take into account the need for Leading and Process indicators:

Leading: Leading indicators tend to be attitudinal, and are about stimulating different conversations, and decision-making frames. Gathering on-going qualitative observations, and reflections can help to make the patterns that inform these indicators clearer.

Process: The forms that process indicators take often differ from organisation to organisation – for example, some organisations might recognise that there is a need to change who is meeting, and how regularly in order to cultivate the right flow of value; some organisations like Spotify have chosen to cancel meetings as they are seen as being a poor substitute for good process.

Outcome: Whilst organisations typically have a collective outcome that they wish to use for monitoring their transformations, teams and groups also have to own their own outcomes. These need to be coherent to the collective, but not controlled.

We introduced the vector-based theory of change in Chapter 2 as an approach to managing emergent change. Emergent change encourages us to maintain a general attitude of adaptability and response-ability. Planned approaches work well in closed-loop complicated systems, however monitoring and measuring change in a complex and ever-emergent system means we cannot define a future state. Outcome indicators are therefore problematic in helping us to understand impact on the system if they are the only guiding indicators in use. In fact, they can also drive the wrong behaviours as we have seen in the cases outlined earlier. Here, we would like to call into effect Goodhart's law, "when a measure becomes a target, it ceases to be a good measure".

Often, in our drive to become data-driven and outcome-driven in business transformation, it tends to pertúrbate the system and cause people to react in several ways. One of Edward Deming's contemporaries, the statistician Donald Wheeler explains that when targets or outcomes are set, and people are placed under pressure to meet them, there are three possible ways that they can proceed. First, people can work to improve the system they are in to achieve these targets. This is the effect we are hoping to achieve with most transformation. However, there are also two other potential ways that targets can be met: they can either distort the system (without effecting the type of change you are seeking) to meet targets, or they can distort the data [42, 43]. The distortion in the system and the data are often experienced as intended consequence of most change and transformation efforts. This helps to explain the importance of factoring Goodhart's law into how we measure and monitor change and progress.

The Four Forms of Goodhart's Law

Whilst Goodhart's law is useful to help us understand the need to rethink how we set targets and monitor change, it is not in and of itself instructive enough to help us understand how to do so. In 2019, researchers David Manheim and Scott Garrabant expanded on this further to outline four common ways in which Goodhart's Law manifests, thereby providing dimensions that can help us better understand how to avoid the errors that Goodhart warns about [44].

These four common forms are:

1. Regressional Goodhart
2. Extremal Goodhart
3. Causal Goodhart
4. Adversarial Goodhart

Regressional Goodhart

Regressional Goodhart can be understood as the issues we experience with setting any targets in complex adaptive systems because of the fact that all measures are at best proxies. Unlike closed-state engineering systems where we can peg the system of units down to clear measures, complex human systems do not have the equivalent of an International System of Units. Regressional Goodhart is therefore impossible to avoid in human systems because nearly every measurement you can think of is an imperfect reflection of the true thing you want to measure.

Earlier in this chapter, we painted this through the example of the call centre striving to achieve performance improvement through average call time to ensure that they are able to support a higher number of customers. This might lead to more calls being answered, and more people's cases being logged, but might inadvertently lead to more calls, but also more unsatisfied customers who had their calls cut short to satisfy a KPI, but not their problems answered. This is a problem that many change agents have experienced, and Manheim and Garrabant warns that whilst it is the most fundamental issue, it is also unavoidable as "an inexact metric necessarily leads to a divergence between the goal and the metric in the tail".

Extremal Goodhart

Extremal Goodhart is a further variation of the issue with proxies as measures that we discussed in Regression – that we use proxies because what we want to measure is not easily measured, and we pick these proxies based on average data. However, at the extreme values of this proxy, some of the relationships between the proxy and the target begin to break down.

A simple example would be the correlation between basketball players and height. Most NBA players are very tall, and the data would suggest that to build a good team, we should look for the tallest person in the world. As skills are not easy to quantify, height becomes one of the early filtering measures. However, as we begin to work with the team, we realise that the tallest person also had issues with walking as his height was due to a pituitary gland issue. At the extremes of the height proxy, our correlation falls apart as it is not able to distinguish between "good outliers" and "bad outliers".

To paint a business example, let us go back to our call centre. As a measure, average call time might provide some useful reflection of performance in average case calls. However, when we are dealing with extreme cases this correlation might fall apart. Across the world, there has been a huge uptick in the number of scam and fraud. Imagine a scam or fraud customer calling the bank to report on such cases. The correlation begins to fall apart as the shortest call time might actually be the worst for the phenomenon, and a long call time with many layers of escalation might be the right approach.

This variation of Goodhart deals with the fact that we tend to pick measures and goals that present correlation in normal situations. However, in adopting these measures, the system begins to optimise for that measure, and as we reach the extreme ends of the measure, the relationship with our goals break down.

Causal Goodhart

This variation of Goodhart's Law is probably the one that is most easy to understand as it points to the problem of mistaking correlation for causation. In transformation journeys, this could be the error of selecting a measure that we believe produces a desired outcome, when actually the two are merely correlated, and that the effects may have been caused by a third or multiple factors. In transformation journeys, false causality makes us optimise for one measure, and then realise that it does not have the causal effect on the outcome you want. We might be ignoring other intermediary factors, or intervening only on a negligible aspect of a broader constellation of factors.

For example, there was a period when many businesses were looking to become more innovative as a way to improve their competitiveness. To do this, they looked into industries thought of as innovative and creative such as the arts and entertainment. It was found that there was a high number of people who were trained in the creative arts. As a result, businesses started bringing in training courses and consultants who could "teach creativity" to their employees. Innovation metrics then started to include how much training in creativity was provided by each company, and how many employees had gone through it. This, however, was found to have little impact on contributing to actual innovation.

Further research revealed that the art and entertainment industries provided a clear coalescent point for those schooled in creative arts, rather than was caused by it. Innovation it was found had more to do with designing for propinquity between different parts of the organisation to encourage greater exchange and cross-pollination, as well latitude from the system. The layering on of training in "creative thinking" was the result of a false causal relationship with innovation. Without changing the conditions around decision-making and exchange in the system, creative thinking became just another distraction and elective training option.

Adversarial Goodhart

Adversarial Goodhart is a variation that is similar to the Cobra effect in British India, as well as the Opium effect in America-occupied

Afghanistan, where actors begin gaming the system and using the metric against the program set up to manage it. Manheim and Garrabant also describe how Adversarial Goodhart results as a combination of agents either exploiting the metric to "create extremal Goodhart effects, or by exacerbating always-present regressional Goodhart, or due to causal intervention by the agent" [44].

A variation of Goodhart's Law is Campbell's Law that describes the corruption and distortion pressures of social indicators: "the more any quantitative social indicator is used for social decision-making, the more subject it will be to corruption pressures and the more apt it will be to distort and corrupt the social processes it is intended to monitor". Further describing the issues with imagining straightforward transformation in human systems.

What Do We Do About It?

Knowing the issues with measurement and indicators helps us appreciate the importance of better indicator design. To correct this, Manheim and Garrabant suggest looking for the truest metric for performance. This might mean that we have to consistently update our measurement systems. However, given that metrics often provide a frame or reference and a common perspective inside your organisation around performance, a constantly shifting goal post can present as conflict. We will have to manage and communicate the need for consistent updating across the organisation for this to be successful.

We have also steadily observed the planning cycles for organisations becoming shorter. Annual plans and targets are no longer as useful as the world shifts so rapidly, and being responsive is critical. Setting high-level goals annually, but shifting into quarterly planning and review cycles has also become the norm, and performance targets require latitude that account for regular updates.

Another approach that is suggested by Intel CEO, Andy Grove, in his book *High Output Management* [45] is to pair indicators as a way to balance distortion in behaviour and data. For example, he suggests that if you want to increase the rate of engineering and release of updates in a technical environment, the measure of rate of increase should also be paired with the rate of bugs reported. In the call centre environment we described, it might be measuring the average call time with the number of repeat calls around the same support ticket. On a strategic and business planning level we see this in the need to balance between short-term needs (the "keep the lights on" business-as-usual priorities in the 2nd Horizon in the Three Horizons Framework), as well as long-term transformational needs (the visionary "business-of-the-future" priorities in the 1st Horizon in the Three Horizons Framework).

A Body of Indicators

Building on Grove's suggestion, for complex adaptive systems, we recommend a combination of metrics that factor in leading, process and outcome indicators so they can capture across temporality and the system.

We shared this image representing the vector theory of change in Chapter 2. It illustrates the way change needs to be made across a portfolio of interventions that are coherent to the desired outcomes. This portfolio will encompass a body of experiments that are designed based on shifting conditions and parts of the process to stimulate change. However, we are mindful that we cannot engineer the said change – the selection and combination of conditions and process changes might be coherently linked to a desired set of outcomes, but we are mindful that they remain hypotheses to be tested, and that waiting for outcomes might be too long a feedback cycle.

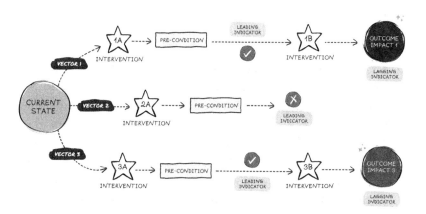

Figure 2.8 Vector Theory of Change depicts identifying possible vectors of change from Chapter 2. It presents a portfolio of interventions based on the possibilities presented by the current state, whilst maintaining mindfulness of the need to manage constraints and pre-conditions.

We, therefore, need to design for leading indicators that can provide early signals on whether interventions are working or not.

In Wheeler's book, *Understanding Variance*, he identifies two different types of studies and data we utilise when managing change. The first is experimental data, referring to "a finite amount of data to perform a one-time analysis while looking for differences that we have tried to create by means of the experiment", and the second is observational data, referring to "a conservative, sequential analysis technique... using a continuing stream of data while looking for signals of any unknown or unplanned change which may occur". The issue with how we have designed for our transformation journeys is that we mistake the first data required for the experimental study with outcome targets.

Experiments that are focused on outcomes, which are usually longer term effects, tend to have longer feedback loops. Such experiments run the risk of being too big to be considered genuine experiments anymore. If they are successful, this is great; however, if they aren't, and trigger negative consequences, the long feedback loop also means we cannot adapt or try to dampen the negative effects in a timely manner. Earlier in this chapter, we discussed the issue with how we pilot change programs, and the issues that occur with traditional thinking around scale. When pilots are overly focused on specific targets they also become easy to game (Goodhart's Law). Leading indicators help us to develop shorter feedback loops, and to manage these effects better.

Whilst organisations tend to prefer a sexy, quantitative metric that presents with more precision and objectivity, Regressional Goodhart has helped us understand that all metrics in human systems are at best rough proxies. And, any change and transformation journey is a journey of subjective sensemaking. It is, therefore, useful to pair quantitative metrics with qualitative data such as customer experience or employee voice.

The stories people tell about their experiences of the system tend to change far more quickly than they show up on any metric. Qualitative data tend to provide a useful lead indicator.

As the quality of the experience shifts, and deeper sensemaking is triggered after early intervention efforts, we can then observe how our broader body of process indicators (or observational data in Wheeler's language) are shifting. The stories and descriptions of changing experience provide a frame with which we can more meaningfully interpret any change in our process indicators.

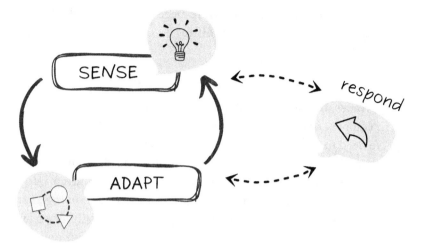

Figure 3.4 Sense-Adapt-Respond from Chapter 3, where Sense-Adapt is presented as a more tightly coupled loop as organisations are continuously learning and adapting.

In Chapter 3 we discussed the Sense-Adapt-respond loop that allows for more adaptive change, with the Sense-Adapt loop being more tightly coupled loop as organisations are continuously learning and adapting. In our sensemaking through change and transformation, it is these qualitative differences that first provide people with data for their sensing. The process indicators that have been identified to accompany that change can then be monitored further. Process data can come from operational measures (i.e. average call time, number of sales made, frequency of exchange and interaction across departments and silos).

Quoting W. Edward Deming, "every system is perfectly designed to get the outcomes that it gets". To do proper systems transformation, therefore, we need to develop a more thorough rethink of what we are monitoring and measuring, and also allow for latitude to account for the emergence that arises in complex adaptive systems. Outcomes are useful to provide a guiding principle, but we need to consistently factor in the sensemaking of agents within the system, as well as the "Voice of the Process". Outcome indicators tend to lag. It takes time, for example, to develop proper reports on things like deals closed or customer satisfaction results. These longer lead times mean these results can guide how we make decisions but tend to only deliver feedback at a later point, and are also subject to all sorts of attributional errors. We therefore need a body of indicators to help us monitor how things are shifting.

Main Take-aways

- Whilst we need to be guided by some loose framework of intended outcomes, organisations need to be mindful that any intervention in complex adaptive systems will create unintended outcomes.
- We need to become more open to different forms of feedback and data as relying on numbers alone is often misleading and distorts the picture. Indicators require more nuance, and nesting into a body of indicators that can be meaningfully understood together.
- Interventions take time to show "outcomes", especially when we understand that we cannot engineer toward a prescriptive outcome or end state when the goal should be to encourage evolvability. We need to identify a body of leading, process and outcome indicators that help us to monitor the evolvability of the system as it is adapting and adjusting.

Meaningful Transformations

In this chapter, we discussed three main sensemaking gaps that are useful to close to improve the organisation's evolvability, as well as some ways of paying forward and paying back on the debt that they create. At the heart of these is the recognition that organisations are human systems that comprise of human beings who require meaning, and a way to reconcile change to what they are used to. There has been a lot written about technical debt and organisational debt by now. Here, we want to highlight the sensemaking gaps that need to be addressed to make transformation meaningful for the people.

We mentioned Robert McNamara earlier, and his strong belief that all systems can, and should be managed through objective and rational analysis. When he died at the ripe age of 93 in 2009, and had an opportunity to reflect on his long life, his obituary in the Economist records that "he was haunted by the thought that amid all the objective-setting and evaluating, the careful counting and the cost-benefit analysis, stood the ordinary human beings. They simply behave unpredictably" [46, 47].

Whilst transformations are often the result of careful analysis and planning, it is not cold rationality that appeals to people. It might help to begin with addressing the business objectives – but people have to be able to reconcile it with their own day-to-day lives and we need to help them along.

NOTE

1 With huge thanks and credit to Steve Schefer who manages the blog *Squire to the Giants*. The inspiration for this reference to Seddon's "roll-in" philosophy was inspired by the blogpost "Rolling, rolling, rolling…" (https://squiretothegiants.com/2015/09/19/rolling-rolling-rolling/?wref=tp).

REFERENCES

[1] Marc Kirschner & John Gerhart. (21 Jul 1998) "Evolvability", in *Proceedings of National Academy of Science USA* (95: 15, 8420–8427).

[2] Michele-Lee Moore, Darcy Riddell & Dana Vocisano. (2015) "Scaling out, scaling up, scaling deep: Strategies of nonprofits in advancing systemic social innovation", in *The Journal of Corporate Citizenship* (58, 67–84).

[3] Karen O'Brien, Rosario Carmona, Irmelin Gram-Hanssen, Gail Hochachka, Linda Sygna & Milda Rosenberg. (May 2023) "Fractal approaches to scaling transformations to sustainability", in *AMBIO A Journal of the Human Environment* (52: 9, 1448–1461).

[4] Marc Schut, Cees Leeuwis & Graham Thiele. (2020) "Science of scaling: Understanding and guiding the scaling of innovation for societal outcomes", in *Agricultural Systems* (184, 102908).

[5] David P.M. Lam, Berta Martın-Lopez, Arnim Wiek, Elena M. Bennett, Niki Frantzeskaki, Andra-Ioana Horcea-Milcu & David J. Lang. (2020) "Scaling the impact of sustainability initiatives: A typology of amplification processes", in *Urban Transformations* (2: 3, 1–24).

[6] Francis Westley, Nino Antadze, Darcy J. Riddell, Kirsten Robinson & Sean Geobey. (2014) "Five configurations for scaling up social innovation: Case examples of nonprofit organisations from Canada", in *The Journal of Applied Behavioural Science* (50, 234–260).

[7] Anna Tsing. (2019) "On non-scalability: The living world is not amenable to precision-nested scales", in *Common Knowledge* (18: 3, 505–524).

[8] Clifford Geertz. (1968) *Peddlers and Princes: Social Development and Economic Change in Two Indonesian Towns.* University of Chicago Press.

[9] Airi Lampinen, Chiara Rossitto & Christofer Gradin Franzén. (25 Oct 2019) "Scaling out, scaling down: Reconsidering growth in grassroots initiatives"', in *Ethnographies of Collaborative Economies Conference Proceedings.* Eds. P. Travlou & L. Ciolfi. University of Edinburgh. Paper No. 2.

[10] Anna Tsing. (2015) *The Mushroom at the End of the World: On the Possibility of Life in Capitalist Ruins.* Princeton University Press.

[11] Danny Hillis. (2016) "The enlightenment is dead, long live the entanglement", in *Journal of Design Science.* https://doi.org/10.21428/1a042043

[12] International Association of Oil & Gas Producers. *About Us.* Accessed 2 Dec 2023. https://www.iogp.org/about-us/

[13] The Sustainable Shipping Initiative. *History.* Accessed 2 Dec 2023. https://www.sustainableshipping.org/about-the-ssi/our-history/

[14] UNDP Strategic Innovation. "Power, politics and transformation", in *Medium.* Accessed 2 Dec 2023. https://medium.com/@undp.innovation/power-politics-and-systems-transformation-182848de225b

[15] Tendayi Viki. "In defence of middle managers who stifle innovation", in *Forbes.* Accessed 2 Dec 2023. https://www.forbes.com/sites/tendayiviki/2017/07/30/in-defence-of-middle-managers-who-stifle-innovation/?sh=8e4145939ee1

[16] Systems Innovation Initiative. "The Deeper Shift: Culture and system change", in *Learning Festival 2020.* Accessed 2 Dec 2023. https://www.systeminnovation.org/festival2020-the-deeper-shift-culture-and-systems-change

[17] Unilever. *Our History and Archives, 2010–2020.* Accessed 2 Dec 2023. https://www.unilever.com/our-company/our-history-and-archives/2010-2020/

[18] Guardian. (5 Oct 2011) "Unilever sustainable living plan". Accessed 2 Dec 2023. https://www.theguardian.com/sustainable-business/unilever-sustainable-living-plan

[19] Forum for the Future. "25 years of visionary collaboration with Unilever". Accessed 2 Dec 2023. https://www.forumforthefuture.org/25-years-of-visionary-collaboration-with-unilever

[20] John Seddon. (2010) "Forget your people - real leaders act on the system", in *Management Innovation eXchange.* Accessed 3 Dec 2023. https://www.managementexchange.com/story/forget-your-people-real-leaders-act-system

[21] John Seddon. (2003) *Freedom from Command and Control: A Better Way to Make the Work.* Vanguard Press.

[22] Dan Breznitz. (2021) *Innovation in Real Places: Strategies for Prosperity in an Unforgiving World.* Oxford University Press.

[23] Richard Holmes. (2008) "A meander through memory and forgetting", in *Memory: An Anthology.* Eds. Harriet Harvey Wood & A.S. Byatt. Chatto and Windus. 95–112.

[24] Amit Jain & Bruce Kogut. (Mar–Apr 2014) "Memory and organizational evolvability in a neutral landscape", in *Organization Science* (25: 2, 479–493).

[25] Steve Blank. (May 2015) "Organizational debt is like technical debt – but worse", in *Forbes* online. https://www.forbes.com/sites/steveblank/2/?015/05/18/organizational-debt-is-like-technical-debt-but-worse-2/??sh=5fe686ac7b35

[26] Aaron Dignan. (June 2016) "How to eliminate organisational debt", in *The Ready Blog.* Accessed 17 Jan 2023.

[27] Damien Mecheri. (2019) *The Works of Fumito Ueda: A Different Perspective on Video Games,* 3rd Editions.

[28] Cynthia J. Bean & Frank E. Hamilton. (2006) "Leader framing and follower sensemaking: Response to downsizing in the brave new workplace", in *Human Relations* (59: 3, 321–349).

[29] Karl E. Weick, K.N. Sutcliffe & D. Obstfeld. (2005) "Organizing and the process of sensemaking", in *Organization Science* (16: 4, 409–421).

[30] Cathrine Filstad. (2014) "The politics of sensemaking and sensegiving at work", in *Journal of Workplace Learning* (26: 1, 3–21).

[31] Andrew Curry & Anthony Hodgson. (2008) "Seeing in multiple horizons: Connecting futures to strategy", in *Journal of Future Studies* (13: 1, 1–20).

[32] Daniel Christian Wahl. (7 June 2017) "The Three Horizons of innovation and culture change", in *Regenerate the Future*. Accessed 27 Dec 2023. https://medium.com/activate-the-future/the-three-horizons-of-innovation-and-culture-change-d9681b0e0b0f

[33] Andrew Curry, Anthony Hodgson, Rachel Kelnar & Alister Wilson. (2006) *Intelligent Infrastructure Systems: The Scenarios - Towards 2055*. Foresight Programme.

[34] Bill Sharpe, Anthony Hodgson, Graham Leicester, Andrew Lyon & Ioan Fazey. (2016) "Three Horizons: A pathways practice for transformation", in *Ecology and Society* (21: 2, 47).

[35] Bill Sharpe, Anthony Hodgson & Ian Page. (2006) "Energy security and climate change", Discussion Paper from *International Futures Forum*, Aberdour.

[36] Phil Rosenzweig. (Dec 2010) "Robert S. McNamara and the evolution of modern management", in *Harvard Business Review Magazine* (88: 12, 9).

[37] Robert McNamara. (1996) *In Retrospect: The Tragedy and Lessons of Vietnam*. Knopf Doubleday Publishing Group.

[38] Daniel Yankelovich. (1972) *Corporate Priorities: A Continuing Study of the New Demands on Business*. Yankelovich Inc.

[39] U.S Government Printing office. (10 Aug 2009) *Afghanistan's Narco War; Breaking the Links between Drug Traffickers and Insurgents*. A report to the Committee of Foreign Relations United States Senate 111th Congress.

[40] Neo Wee Na. (2018) "Opium production and countering terrorism financing in Afghanistan: Lessons from Thailand's royal projects", in *Counter Terrorist Trends and Analyses* (10: 2, 1–5).

[41] Josh Meyer. (8 July 2018) "The secret war of how American lost the drug war with the Taliban", in *Politico Investigation*. Accessed 28 Jul 2023. https://www.politico.com/story/2018/07/08/obama-afghanistan-drug-war-taliban-616316

[42] Donald J. Wheeler. (2000) *Understanding Variation: The Key to Managing Chaos*, 2nd edition. SPC Press. ISBN 978-0-945320-53-1.

[43] Cedric Chin. (11 Jan 2023) "Goodhart's Law Isn't as Useful as you might think", in *Commoncog*. Accessed 11 Feb 2024. https://commoncog.com/goodharts-law-not-useful/

[44] David Manheim & Scott Garrabant. (2018) "Categorising variants of Goodhart's Law", in ArXiv (abs/1803.04585).

[45] Andy Grove. (1995) *High Output Management*, 2nd edition. Vintage.

[46] Robert McNamara. (9 July 2009) *The Economist*. Accessed 28 Jul 2023. https://www.economist.com/obituary/2009/07/09/robert-mcnamara

[47] T. Singh & N. Shah. (2023) "Competency-based medical education and the McNamara fallacy: Assessing the important or making the assessed important?", in *Journal of Postgraduate Medicine* (69: 1, 35–40).

Five

Immanent within complex adaptive systems, is evolutionary potential that affords multiple different, but coherent pathways.

Thus far, we have presented this book in a single voice. The product has been a synthesis of both authors' perspectives, experience and thinking. In embrace of the concept of evolvability, in our last chapter, we provide two conclusions. Each written by one of two co-authors.

We started off this book by offering an alternative frame for leaders and managers to make sense of transformation. The metaphor of evolvability implies that organisations are living ecosystems that are consistently in a state of "becoming". Transformation needs to be regarded as part of ongoing and intentional evolution, and any transformation plan needs to recognise the organisation's living and complex adaptive nature. Effective transformation efforts focus on allowing healthy variation and distributed sensemaking of change within loosely aligned strategic direction.

In providing two different but coherent concluding perspectives, we wish to re-iterate the importance of mutation, adaptation and coherent diversity in navigating transformation, and allowing for evolvability.

CONCLUSION – IN SUNIL'S WORDS

Change initiatives are commonly called "digital transformation," though, as this report outlines, successful transformation is not a one-time change or single new technology adoption. Rather, it requires the organisation to acquire the ability to continuously adapt to change. Although many organisations have the digital fundamentals in place, an updated tech stack and agile IT frameworks are just the beginning. Instead, change should be an evolutionary process that's built into the organisation's mission and every aspect of its operations and strategy. [1]

The Need to Look beyond Traditional Approach to Transformation

It appears that almost every enterprise, regardless of industry and geography, is implementing a Transformation initiative. However, the

DOI: 10.4324/9781003505433-6

data which is consistently coming out from multiple empirical studies paint a dismal picture on the success rates of transformation initiatives, viz. less than 30%. Clearly, something is going wrong big time.

There are three primary themes why transformations are failing.

Lack of Intrinsic Alignment/Commitment among Senior Leadership

This usually happens when a decision has been made at the top, by the Board of Directors or the CEO, and the senior leadership is expected to jump onboard.

The underlying reasons are many – "why change when we are doing well now," "what's in it for me, especially since I am so close to retirement", feeling insecure about the change, fearing loss of power and control, etc.

Merely Tinkering with Change

Given that Transformation has become a buzzword, it means almost everyone wants to jump on the bandwagon. It comes in many forms – Agile Transformation, Digital Transformation and Enterprise Transformation are some of the popular variants. However, the scope of change is extremely limited, often only to the IT function and furthermore limited to merely adopting agile ways of working. Very few enterprises are taking the bold steps needed to transform the entire organisation. Continuing to use the bell curve for individual performance evaluation where the outcome is driven by a cross functional team and having an annual budgeting process that relies on forecasting accuracy in a fast-changing environment are some common examples of areas which are untouched and yet leaders declaring the transformation as complete and successful.

Lack of Understanding of the Nature of Organisational Change

A commonly used metaphor for Transformation is that of a caterpillar turning into a butterfly. It's important to understand that metamorphosis as a process is not trivial. It's essentially a rebirth into something new. And the process of rebirth is painful, like it is for the caterpillar. It involves breaking away from existing paradigms so is highly disruptive as well.

Unfortunately, it is quite common to see so-called transformation initiatives that, metaphorically, are trying to make the caterpillar run faster which it just does not have the capability to do, or worse, unintentionally injuring the caterpillar in a bid to transform it.

Enterprises and their leaders often completely underestimate the time, effort and costs involved in transforming an enterprise. One often wonders whether the leaders understand the meaning and implications of what a metamorphosis means. The underlying thinking towards transformations largely is that the enterprise is like a close ended and mechanistically modelled system, where there is a tight linear relationship between interventions and consequences, the behaviour of system components is certain and predictable and where problems can be solved by taking a reductionist approach.

This mindset manifests in following anti patterns:

- Declaring a transformation completion date in advance, and working backwards from that date.
- Announcing a transformation as successful on seeing some "green shoots", which will get killed by the antibodies arising from the interventions and/or the inertia from the rest of the enterprise which has not changed. This has led to a new person coming in and announcing a fresh transformation initiative, after the regression of the green shoots, thereby causing change fatigue in the enterprise.
- Assuming change can be implemented top down, thereby getting compliance but not necessarily commitment.
- Sticking to plan driven change, thereby ignoring emergent responses from the system.
- Copying a framework or an approach to change, without tailoring it to context.

From Metamorphosis to Evolvability

In today's dynamic and highly complex environment, the choice for enterprises is clear – to stay ahead or at least keep up with the pace of change or face the risk of becoming irrelevant or even extinct.

In my experience, Transformation initiatives are designed on the core principles of metamorphosis, viz.

- Moving the entity from one fixed state to another fixed state.
- Executed as a one-time initiative.

Given the high failure rates of transformation initiatives, the question to ponder over is whether a metamorphosis type of transformation is always the appropriate model for bringing in change in enterprises or if there is a better alternative.

Before attempting to address the question, let's examine the implications of metamorphosis type of transformative change for enterprises.

Emergence can Invalidate the Transformation Plan and Underlying Assumptions

Unlike natural systems where the metamorphosis pathway is built into the DNA of the respective species, transformation in enterprises is not a natural or organic occurrence, as it is based on interventions. The interventions are based on many assumptions, most of which are often implicit. As enterprises are Complex Adaptive Systems (CAS), and any intervention in a CAS is essentially a hypothesis. CAS will respond to interventions with emergent circumstances, including unintended consequences. This can make the planned interventions obsolete or irrelevant. Unless the future interventions are aligned to the new realities arising out of emergence, the transformation initiative is destined to be a train wreck.

It is based on Transition from one Static State to Another Static State

The main characteristic of metamorphosis is that it moves the entity from one static state to another. Hence, most transformation initiatives are just about playing catch up to the current state in the business and environment, which is changing constantly and at an exponential rate. So even assuming that the transformation is successful in terms of reaching the target state, the changed state of the enterprise will become obsolete quickly. The enterprise is once again out of sync with the fast-changing environment.

Disruptive and Risky

Metamorphic change is usually rapid and plan driven, which aligns with enterprises declaring a deadline to complete the transformation. The deadline is often highly unrealistic and is often driven by incentives linked to Transformation being "done". This results in change being pushed top-down disregarding emergence and the appetite for change. This can be quite overwhelming for people across the enterprise, leading to disruptions and loss of morale. Moreover, the urgency can lead to increased risk of failure, especially if the assumptions behind the plan are invalidated due to emergent circumstances.

Loss of Institutional Knowledge

Metamorphosis style of changes involve significant shifts in strategy, structure and ways of working. The basic philosophy is to discard the old and build or move on to something new. In the purest form of metamorphosis, the new state may be completely different from the earlier state, for example the butterfly has no resemblance and characteristics of a caterpillar.

Institutional knowledge often includes an understanding of past successes and failures. Transformation may overshadow or erase the historical context of certain decisions and actions, making it difficult for the organisation to learn from its own experiences.

Because of deadline pressures, knowledge retention and transfer seldom gets the intentionality and priority in most transformation initiatives.

Momentum is Not Sustainable

As stated earlier, metamorphosis is moving an object from a fixed state to another fixed state. The intensity of change is high and often leads to fatigue across the enterprise. However, given the fast-changing environment, the changed state needs to change again to keep with the evolved environment. This often calls for the second wave of transformation initiative to be launched. And these multiple waves create tremendous fatigue and lead people to lose faith in change initiatives and thus become disengaged.

So why does metamorphosis happen consistently and successfully in a biological organism, for example, caterpillar, but not in enterprises?

- Metamorphosis in organisms is governed by a genetic code, which ensures a smooth and successful transition. In cases of enterprises, however, each transformation is unique given that the external and internal factors for a given enterprise are distinctive to that specific enterprise. Moreover, due to the genetic code, as painful as the metamorphosis may be, the organism does not face the inertia to change, which enterprises unavoidably do.

- A biological organism is not dependent on any external factor for the metamorphosis, but an enterprise's transformation involves many external entities, viz. customers, partners, shareholders, etc.
- An organism's metamorphosis is an individual journey, with each organism undergoing the same predetermined sequence. In contrast, enterprise transformation involves a collective shift – changing the behaviours, mindsets and skills of numerous individuals at once. The diversity in terms of pace of change across different stakeholder groups can prove very challenging.

By no means am I suggesting that metamorphosis transition types of change are not needed or don't work. For example, during the Covid pandemic, enterprises across industries and geographies had to quickly adapt and come up with innovative ways of engaging with and delivering products and services to their customers. Many enterprises pivoted their business models, the most prominent pattern was having a brick-and-mortar presence to having a strong digital presence and patterning with complimentary service providers. Restaurants were a prime example of this. A major transformative and irreversible change which has happened across the globe is people being able to work from home, especially in knowledge work industries. And this change was not just at a physical level, but also at the mindset level.

Adapting to the need to work from home is a great example of how change can happen swiftly, when the existence is threatened, which is the case for almost all types of enterprises. Something which was deemed as impractical or even impossible before Covid had to be done just to ensure survival. It clearly showcases that when faced with an existential threat, an enterprise can achieve deep and outcome-oriented change through quickly making strategic shifts, acting decisively, with speed and changing the mindsets. Examples include an insurance company in Australia, which acquired another insurance company twice its size and started crumbling under its new weight. The company underwent a metamorphosis change including creating a new technology-based platform, redefining their product strategy and moving to a culture of employee empowerment.

Another example is Lego, facing the reality of fast declining sales decided to embrace digitization. They launched successful video games and animated movies, expanding their brand beyond physical bricks. They also invested in educational robotics and STEM toys, aligning with modern learning trends.

So, while a metamorphosis approach to change/transformations may work under certain circumstances, this approach is not effective to enable enterprises to deal with an exponentially and continuously fast changing environment.

Unlike biological metamorphosis, which relies on the blueprint of genetic code for a predictable transformation, enterprises lack such inherent guidance. Each transformation is unique and requires tailored strategies based on individual circumstances. To treat a journey of change which needs constant adjustments and refinements like a singular event is a recipe for failure.

Thinking in terms of fixed states is like building a sandcastle on the beach. The tide of change will inevitably wash it away. The environment evolves too quickly for metamorphosis type of change.

To summarise, traditional, "big bang" transformation efforts – akin to the dramatic metamorphosis of a caterpillar into a butterfly – are ill-equipped to navigate the constant churn of technological advancements, shifting market dynamics, and ever-evolving customer expectations. Instead, what's needed is a shift in mindset, a move from episodic change to cultivating the internal capability for continuous evolution.

CHARACTERISTICS OF CONTINUOUS EVOLUTION

What does continuous evolution look like in practice? Unlike the static "before and after" of metamorphosis, it has several unique characteristics.

Iterative and Incremental

Continuous evolution thrives on small, experimental improvements, tested and refined in real-time. It is like a climber ascending a mountain, taking one measured step at a time, adapting to the terrain, and adjusting their route as needed. This iterative approach minimises risk, fosters learning, and allows for quicker course correction.

Continuous and Ongoing

Evolution doesn't happen in discrete bursts. It's a constant process, interwoven into the fabric of the organisation's operations. It's about building a culture of experimentation and learning, where feedback loops are short, and insights are acted upon swiftly. Every interaction and touchpoint become an opportunity to learn, evolve and improve.

Leveraging Learnings and Retaining Knowledge

Unlike the clean slate of metamorphosis, continuous evolution builds on the past. Institutional knowledge and accumulated learnings are invaluable assets, not relics to be discarded. The challenge lies in capturing and disseminating these learnings effectively, ensuring they inform future iterations and guide the ongoing adaptation.

Ongoing Refinement and Adaptation

In today's context change is the only constant. What works today may not be relevant tomorrow. Continuous evolution necessitates a relentless pursuit of refinement and adaptation. Processes, strategies, and even organisational structures must be flexible enough to bend with the shifting winds of change. This requires a commitment to achieve and maintain a high level of agility across the enterprise.

The transition from metamorphosis to continuous evolution is not merely a tactical shift; it's a fundamental change in how organisations perceive and respond to the world around them. It's about embracing uncertainty, learning from experience, and enhancing agility. By cultivating this evolutionary capability, organisations can thrive in an ever-changing world, staying ahead of the curve and continuously pushing the boundaries of what's possible.

IMPLICATIONS FOR LEADERSHIP

Leadership is about having the influence to change, and is not about position and power, even though there may be a high degree of correlation between position and power, and influence in many enterprises.

Here are some potential implications for leadership for enabling evolvability.

Reframing Leadership as Orchestrators of Change

Shift from imposing top-down transformations to facilitating emergent change. Give people the space and tools to experiment, adapt and solve problems on the fly.

Cultivate a culture of learning and curiosity. Encourage questioning, exploration and small-scale experiments. Make failure a learning experience, not a stigma.

Embrace decentralisation and distributed decision-making. Break down the hierarchy walls — let ideas flow freely, not just through the chain of command. Trust your team to make decisions on the front lines, and watch innovation take off.

Building and Sustaining Evolutionary Capabilities

Invest in fostering enterprise level agility. Encourage cross-functional collaboration, rapid prototyping and iterative development, to get fast feedback. Break down silos and create seamless information flow.

Develop the "adaptive muscle" of your workforce. Equip individuals with the skills and mindsets needed for continuous learning, problem-solving and embracing ambiguity.

Integrate learning and feedback loops into the fabric of daily operations. Use data like a spotlight to guide decisions and refine your approach on the fly.

Walk the Talk, be the Change You Want to See

Demonstrate a growth mindset by embracing challenges and continuous learning. Show that you're not afraid to roll up your sleeves and learn new things. Embrace challenges as opportunities to grow and be open to feedback that makes you a better leader.

Communicate the vision and importance of continuous evolution clearly and consistently. Paint a clear picture of the future, where change is the norm, not the exception. Align individual actions with that vision, making everyone feel like part of the bigger evolution.

Champion and celebrate small wins and incremental progress. Recognise the value of continuous learning and adaptation, not just grand transformations.

Pivot Measurement and Success

Move beyond traditional metrics of success that focus on one-time transformations. Embrace metrics that track the ability to adapt, bounce back and learn from curveballs.

Foster the ability to deal with unexpected challenges. Celebrate the ability to respond to change, not just hitting predefined targets.

Think marathon, not sprint – prioritise long-term sustainability and adaptability over short-term gains and quick fixes.

Acknowledge the challenges of shifting from interventional and episodic change to continuous evolution. Change is a bumpy ride, own it. Expect some folks to cling to the old ways at least for a while and be ready to offer support and a helping hand. Remember that not everyone will change at the same pace.

Provide support and resources for individuals and teams making the transition. Make them feel like co-pilots, not passengers, on this evolutionary journey.

Communicate the long-term benefits of continuous evolution. Show the light at the end of the tunnel – paint a picture of a company that's resilient, relevant and always one step ahead of the competition.

IN SUMMARY

The tide of change is rising, disrupting industries and ecosystems. Relying on one-time "transformations" – akin to a caterpillar's dramatic but singular metamorphosis – is to invite irrelevance and eventual extinction. The future belongs to those who embrace the relentless current of evolution, weaving agility into the very fabric of their existence.

Think of change not as a grand spectacle event, but as a continuous ascent – one measured step at a time. Each experiment, each failure, each feedback loop fuels the climb, propelling organisations upwards towards new heights. This is continuous evolution, an ongoing tryst with the ever-shifting winds of the environment.

Leaders are no longer architects of grand blueprints, but skilled orchestrators of this dynamic dance. They cultivate a culture of curiosity, where questioning becomes the norm and failure a stepping stone. They break down the rigid walls of hierarchy, allowing ideas to flow freely, nurtured by the cross-pollination of diverse perspectives. Every employee, empowered and equipped, becomes a micro-pilot in the journey, guiding the organisation towards ever-evolving shores.

Continuous evolution demands new metrics – not a scorecard of one-time wins, but a compass that tracks the organisation's ability to learn, adapt and bounce back from adversity. It celebrates the nimbleness on uncertain terrain, the resilience to weather unexpected storms, the relentless pursuit of progress even in the face of headwinds.

This shift is not easy. It requires unlearning old habits, dismantling obsolete mindsets, and embracing the discomfort of constant change. But the rewards are worth the struggle. Imagine an organisation that thrives on uncertainty, constantly reinventing itself, leaving competitors in awe. This is the legacy of continuous evolution, the mark of those who dare to ride the wave of change, becoming not just survivors, but architects of a brighter future.

The choice is stark: Metamorphosis or Evolvability? Choose metamorphosis and face the risk of becoming a relic of a bygone era. Choose evolvability and thrive, not just survive, in a fast changing and disruptive environment. The future belongs to those enterprises which have the capability to evolve continuously.

CONCLUSION – IN ZHEN'S WORDS

Systems are either **optimising** to reduce variation after repeated processes of natural selection, or **adapting** to produce variability and mutating for novel traits, or in select cases, are **'frozen accidents'** (because natural selection works with the best available at the time, not the best possible).[1]

We began in Chapter 1 with a discussion around the changing metaphors of organisation that we have been observing. We discussed how we have gone from a more mechanistic framing that describes organisations as consisting of a series of levers that can be pulled to bring about the changes one wishes to see; to one that regards organisations as living systems, enmeshed within an even broader ecosystem of competitors, supply chains, customers, partners and network effects. Change within this living systems metaphor has often been framed as organisational evolution.

Evolvability: Organisational Capability and Propensity for Adaptation
The concept of organisational evolution borrows concepts and thinking from evolutionary biology. However, the popular frames of organisational evolution tend to be maturity frameworks that still continue to present transformation as organisations going from one static state, to another preferred state of homeostasis. Whilst living systems can

achieve stable states, they are never static. Or, as Karl Weick puts more eloquently, "rather than moving from one stable state to another discrete point, change is consistently unfolding and experienced as an emergent flow of possibilities, and a conjunction of events and open-ended interactions occurring over time". Organisations are therefore always optimising or adapting in response to the on-going flow of change, and can never lock into stasis if they wish to survive.

Another popular evolutionary frame is the Darwinian concept of "survival of the fittest". This concept was interpreted as on-going competition, and for a long time this understanding dominated strategic thinking. This "competition" puts all organisations in a steady state of evolution as they try to learn and out-do one another. Whilst competition for resources and access do exert evolutionary pressures, this interpretation of "survival of the fittest" is an incomplete one. In his own explanations, Darwin notes that animals all co-evolve in response to each other. Survival, however, also requires us to co-evolve with the systems we interact with, and our evolutionary trajectories need to be ever adaptive in order to smartly transform. Research has shown that examples of accelerated evolution and transformation in species, and the rise of dominant species, has more likely been caused by opportunistic moves into new ecological niches, rather than through mere competition alone. Going beyond competition analysis, we also need to broaden our scanning, and sense the environment to identify unforeseen adaptive advantages as they emerge.

The deeper exploration of this metaphor revealed to us that responsiveness and ability to adapt is more critical than mere enhancing of competitiveness. Or, in the words of Darwin: "It is not the strongest of the species that survives, nor the most intelligent, but the one most responsive to change". It is with this understanding that we recognised the importance when managing organisational transformation in a rapidly changing environment, to shift the focus from *evolution* to *evolvability*.

Evolution as a concept places focus on (1) the actual characteristics of the change.[2] Secondarily, it also (2) explores the evolutionary processes which affect the change. We found this to be incomplete as it assumes an end-point as represented by the observable changes. Evolvability, on the other hand, looks at the system's ability and capacity to support on-going adaptive diversity in response to environmental pressures.

Our alternate framing places focus on enhancing organisational *capability*, and *propensity* for *adaptation* because we understand transformation to be a continuous process of adapting to a volatile and uncertain environment.

EVOLVABILITY AND HOW WE FRAME TRANSFORMATION

In exploring evolvability as a concept for transformation, we reviewed the difference between planned and emergent change, and how this influences different approaches to planning. Most strategies for change are designed by identifying a preferred state or outcomes for a targeted point in the future. Plans are then made that help to roadmap the journey from where we are today to that envisioned future state. The visualisation that is commonly used to demonstrate this type of change greatly resembles a directional curve in micro-evolution (see Figure 5.1).

In a paper published in *Genetica* in 2001, Arnold, Pfender and Jones describe three archetypal curves that act as conceptual bridges between micro, localised evolution and macroevolution [2]. Whereas, microevolution refers to small changes over short periods of time. Macroevolution refers to larger changes over a much longer time

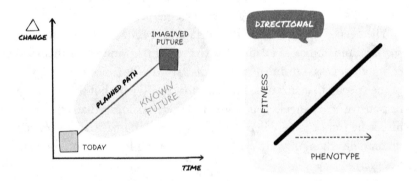

Figure 5.1 Linear Path to Change (left) depicts a common planning map of desired change over time. **Directional Monotonic Curve (right)** depicts a linear direction of change that can either increase or decrease in fitness over time. This type of curve tends to correspond to a pattern of selection where one extreme phenotype, or pattern is seen as fittest for the system.

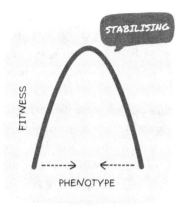
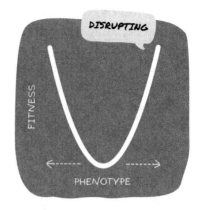

Figure 5.2 Stabilising Curve (left) depicts a selection that seeks to stabilise the evolution when an intermediate phenotype, or pattern is fittest. This implies some synthesis between diverse patterns of change that need to be effectively reconciled. **Disrupting Curve (right)** depicts a selection where two phenotypes are fitter than the intermediate between them, implying the need for the system to diversify.

scale. The directional curve depicts a linear direction of change that can either increase or decrease in fitness over time. This type of curve tends to correspond to a pattern of selection where one extreme phenotype, or pattern is seen as fittest for the system. Most of our planning resembles this linear directional curve. However, the monotonic curve is only 1 of 3 common shapes of microevolution.

The two other curves that could take shape are either a dome-shaped stabilising curve, or a U-shaped disrupting curve.

The stabilising curve corresponds with a selection that seeks to stabilise the evolution when an intermediate phenotype, or pattern is fittest. This implies some synthesis between diverse patterns of change need to be effectively reconciled. Finally, the disrupting curve corresponds to a selection where two phenotypes are fitter than the intermediate between them, implying the need for the system to diversify. Now it is important to note that these explanations and illustrations depict the adaptive landscape of a system only in one, single dimension. Every system comprises multiple dimensions, which at any moment are testing, and trying to identify the best available mutation and change for that system.

To go back to our graph depicting change over time, the planned pathway depicting a simple linear direction of travel is therefore a gross simplification. The reality of transformation is all 3 curves happening repeatedly, across multiple dimensions, seeking to optimise (directional), adapt (stabilising or disrupting) or revealing frozen accidents.

The pathways of change will in all likelihood look more like an entangled web than a directional curve (see Figure 5.3). This is also why in Chapter 2, we remind everyone that there's your roadmap, and then there is what really happens to effect and shepherd transformation. These journeys require organisational commitment to resources, new goals and ways of working that disrupt and incur short-term opportunity costs. Planning is a critical discipline, but plans made at a specific point in time, are incapable of factoring in emergence and all its potential possibilities. The roadmap is a simple story that limits how we scan and plan.

Planning is critical to help us clarify objectives and guidelines that help discipline our efforts and decision-making. However, whilst a lot of intense and intelligent thinking and analysis goes into such endeavours, the reality of transformation journeys is that they often deviate from the roadmap as envisioned. Therefore, whilst planning is critical in transformation journeys, we recognise that shepherding that change will require us to both plan, as well as allow for change to emerge.

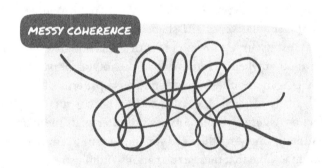

Figure 5.3 Messy Coherence (above) depicts a representation of the way transformational pathways across multiple dimensions in a complex adaptive system are more likely to look.[3]

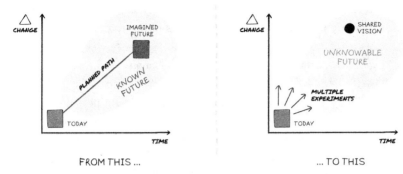

FROM THIS ...   ... TO THIS

Figure 5.4 Planned Path to Change (left) depicts a common planning map of desired change over time which is an unrealistic simple, linear directional representation of transformation. **Adaptive Strategy (right)** depicts a representation of an adaptive strategy toward change which factors in the reality of unknowable future conditions. This means that instead of a set goal that we will arrive at, we need a broader vision that can guide us. This will also be achieved through a broad but coherent body of multiple experiments, rather than a straight and narrow roadmap as depicted in Figure 5.1.[4]

In working with organisations as they navigate transformation and response to an ever-changing environment, we therefore advise and coach that we move from a simple story to a more realistic depiction that broadens our understanding and diversifies our efforts.

A visual understanding of the different curves of evolution that are possible, as well as the realisation that all systems are navigating changes across multiple dimensions at any given time helps us to appreciate how difficult it is to be overly fixated on a plan or predefined outcomes. The best transformation outcomes will come from enhancing the system's adaptive diversity. This will come from cultivating shorter and more responsive feedback loops, recognising the need for experimentation in a complex environment, and dynamic allocation of resources based on feedback across a diversity of indicators. The vision of the future provides a coherent narrative and set of heuristics that can guide decision-making, but must also be broad enough to allow for emergence, and unknown and unknowable outcomes.

Transformation, then, is about building capacity, enhancing conditions and dynamic allocation of resources rather than outcomes.

Evolvability: Organising, Rather Than Organisation

Like the levees constructed to keep out the ravaging forces of the sea, 'organisations' are precarious social constructions designed to temporarily stave off and buffer the effects of relentless change always already taking place regardless of human intentions... Managing change then consists not so much of wilfully imposing our predesigned order onto reality and forcibly making it conform to our will and fancy. Instead, it is about resisting this urge to confront the world head on; to bide our time and let change happen. [3]

Transformation needs to be regarded as a part of on-going change and evolution, and recognise that we are working with a complex human system, embedded within broader emergent systems. It is more effective then, as suggested by Karl Weick, that we think about what we do as "organising", instead of merely referring to the "organisation". He suggests that the word, organisation, is inaccurate as it is a noun. Whereas, organisations are actually in a constant state of flux and process of remaking. Framing it as "organising" helps us to understand the dynamism and the on-going sensemaking that is occurring throughout the system to organise people, communication and behaviour in a manner that represents the organisation.

This sensemaking is the process through which change and adaptation is negotiated, and new practices emerge. It is described as "reciprocal exchanges between actors (Enactment) and their environments (Ecological Change) that are made meaningful (Selection) and preserved (Retention)" [4]. This is the process through which people make sense of change, understand how to act, and what to stop, and decide what endures.

Similarly, a transformation strategy or plan are nouns, and we need to recognise the process of a system making sense of change. Contrary to classical strategy and planning where organisation follows strategy, this age of uncertainty means that transformation requires strategy to remain responsive and adaptive to emergent processes of organising instead. To conduct the best sensing that can guide us in adapting to the shifting environment and evolving landscape of stakeholder and customer needs, in Chapter 3 we discussed the importance of distributing adaptive freedom to the edges of the organisation.

Enhancing agency within enabling constraints, help to keep healthy the metabolic mechanisms needed to maintain evolvability. People need to be empowered and responsible to lead. They need to be able to make decisions, take action and communicate without unwieldy bureaucratic chain-of-command gates. Leaders also need to be able to solicit new ideas at all levels, know when and how to create business proposals, and how to translate new ideas into plans and action. This highlights the porosity of our organisations. Enterprises are complex adaptive systems – they are not closed systems, but are also not without boundaries. The boundaries are porous, and to stimulate the kind of adaptive mutation needed for ongoing evolvability we have to cultivate boundary spanners across all levels that help us to better Sense-Adapt-respond.

The real change tends to happen at the edges, and your people closest to the frontline can best sense this horizon. They have the shortest feedback loops with customers and the evolving situations on the ground. The middle of the organisation needs to provide support and facilitate dynamic allocation of resources and flow of information to support these strategic frontline needs. Your top leaders need to architect something that can support the whole. This approach allows us to enhance organisational evolvability and better activate the four key forces that drive evolution: allow for mutation, stimulate gene flow, bet on natural selection and attune to genetic drift.

Management Professor Robert Chia of the Adam Smith Business School describes this process-approach to organisation as an increasingly necessary frame. "We are living in an era of unprecedented change; one that is characterised by instability, volatility and dramatic transformations. It is a world in which the seemingly improbable, the unanticipated, and the downright catastrophic appear to occur with alarming regularity. Such a world calls for a new kind of thinking: Thinking that issues from the chaotic, fluxing immediacy of lived experiences; thinking that resists or overflows our familiar categories of thought; and thinking that accepts and embraces messiness, contradictions, and change as the sine qua non of the human condition. Thinking in genuinely processual terms means that the starting point of our inquiry is not so much about the being of entities such as 'organisation', but their constant and perpetual becoming" [5].

In such a world, organisations learn to respond more by sensing, improvising and adapting as they go. This is a strategy that emerges from these coping practices, or "strategy-in-practice" as Chia, and his colleagues McKay and Nair refer to them [6]. Change relies more on practice-acquired sensitivities and dispositions. The evolveable organisation therefore recognises that the Sense-Adapt-respond loop has a small "r" that lags the ongoing Sense-Adapt cycle. Whereas, traditional approaches to transformation and strategy have focused more on an organisation's formal "response" to managing in complexity and uncertainty, in evolvability, we recognise the need for multiple, ongoing experiments, as well as differentiated approaches that are nested in a disciplined way across different parts of the business.

EVOLVABILITY: SUSTAINABLE AND REGENERATIVE TRANSFORMATION

I was recently watching a documentary on climbing Mount Everest... they stated that most of the 300 plus deaths that have occurred on Everest happened in the 'Death Zone', the region above 8,000 meters (26k ft.) where the atmospheric pressure is at 30% less than the levels at the base, causing the climbers bodies to literally begin to stop working. The effect of this process is that it takes most climbers up to 12 hours to walk the 1.7 kilometre's (1.07 miles) from Camp 4 to the summit. Exhausted, many climbers simply sit down to rest and drift to sleep, never to wake up again. What is even more astounding about the Death Zone is that a majority of these deaths occur during the descent down the mountain... Sherpa and record holder (25 ascents), Kami Rita claims the descent is the real killer saying, 'When returning, their (the climbers) body is out of energy, and many people die'...

IN THE PLANNING ROOM   THE REALITY OF AN EVOLVING LANDSCAPE

Figure 5.5 Mount Everest Death Zone Comic presents a cartoon depiction of the issues with transformation initiatives that do not plan for the need to sustain their effect.

Hearing this, I began to think of the perils of leading change. I think this is fair considering the number of projects I have seen where the leaders, thinking they are being super creative, use the analogy of climbing Mount Everest to represent their change project journey. In retrospect, what is interesting in their use of this analogy is that they make the same mistake as many climbers, they claim the goal being reached at the summit, not keeping in mind the descent. In other words, they claim victory with the implementation of the change but don't take into account the time between go-live and when outcomes are achieved.

Similarly, success on a project occurs when the metrics show that change has been adopted and will be sustained and the outcomes are being achieved. Focusing on implementation rather than the adoption and achievement of outcomes is the equivalent of forgetting the safe descent on Everest. [7]

This anecdote was shared with me when I was having discussion around gaps in the change management literature with a friend, David Lee. David also happens to be the Managing Director of Prosci Singapore, and writes, teaches and advises specifically on the topic of change and transformation. I cackled when he shared this, and thought it was a wonderful analogy to describe again the importance of focusing on building and enhancing an enterprise's capability for sensing, adapting and responding, and its overall evolvability; rather than fixate on a vision of its next evolution.

Through the course of writing this book, we went through many exchanges and processes of review and consultation with fellow practitioners. One of the comments we had received was a concern that evolvability and its inherent philosophy of allowing for emergent and adaptive strategy might create a "frog in boiling water" effect for many organisations. They were concerned that allowing for the constant sensing and adapting would mean organisations would over time evolve in a way that does not fit the organisation's vision. I thought about this, and my response would be that it is sometimes the predefined strategy that might be causing the organisation to become the frog sitting in boiling water, as a fixed strategy regardless of the wide sea of changes that are happening every given moment might be creating the wrong kind of focus. This also continues to frame transformation as a point to arrive at, rather than the outcome itself.

Change is not an exceptional undertaking, nor a series of projects to complete. Continuous change is reality, transformation is the capability to live and thrive.

At the end of the day just as change is an enduring truth, organisations need to sustainably transform to cultivate the capacity of their systems for regenerative adaptive diversity necessary to keep up with an ever-changing environment.

NOTES

1 In considering how to frame this conclusion, I thought it would be best to go back to the paper that inspired the name of this book: "Evolvability", by Kirschner and Gerhart (1998).
2 Inherited or reproducible traits and characteristics.
3 Image depicting *Messy Coherence* is adapted from Sue Borchadt's illustrations in "Cynefin: Weaving sense-making into the fabric of our world", Cognitive Edge Pte Ltd (page 64)
4 Image depicting *a move from traditional to adaptive strategy* is adapted from Sue Borchadt's illustrations in "Cynefin: Weaving sense-making into the fabric of our world", Cognitive Edge Pte Ltd (page 264)

REFERENCES

[1] MIT Technology Review Insights, in association with Thoughtworks (March 29, 2023) "Evolutionary organizations reimagine the future: Capabilities for continuous reinvention help organizations meet the moment", https://www.technologyreview.com/2023/03/29/1070438/evolutionary-%20organizations-%20reimagine-%20the-%20future (Accessed 24 Sep 2024)
[2] S.J. Arnold, M.E. Pfrender & A.G. Jones. (2001) "The adaptive landscape as a conceptual bridge between micro and macroevolution", in *Genetica* (112–113: 9–32).
[3] Robert Chia. (2014) "Reflections: In praise of silent transformation – allowing change through 'letting happen'", in *Journal of Change Management* (14: 1, 8–27). DOI:10.1080/14697017.2013.841006
[4] K.E. Weick, K.M. Sutcliffe & D. Obstfeld. (2005) "Organizing and the process of sensemaking", in *Organization Science* (16: 4, 409–421). https://doi.org/10.1287/orsc.1050.0133
[5] Ann Langley & Haridimos Tsoukas. "Endorsements", in *Perspectives in Process Organisation Studies Series*. Oxford University Press.
[6] Brian MacKay, Robert Chia & Anup Nair. (2021) "Strategy-inpractices: A process philosophical approach to understanding strategy emergence and organizational outcomes", in *Human Relations* (74: 9, 1337–1369). https://doi.org/10.1177/0018726720929397
[7] David William Lee "Surviving the change death zone", in *David William Lee Writing*. Accessed 24 Feb 2024. https://www.davidleeglobal.com/post/surviving-thechange-deathzone